"No one has chronicled the secrets behind the nation's fastest growing companies the way Skip Weitzen has. This is an easy-to-read how-to manual for achieving hypergrowth. It should be mandatory reading for any CEO or entrepreneur who isn't satisfied with conventional growth."

JOE CAPPO
Publisher, *Advertising Age* and author of *FutureScope*

"Skip Weitzen's ability to define common components for success in the Information Age are uncanny. His observations in *Infopreneurs* defined the burgeoning multi-billion dollar infotext industry before others began to recognize it. With *Hypergrowth* Weitzen has drawn the treasure map that will guide the enterprising business explorer to new lands of achievement."

RICK PARKHILL, President
InfoText Publishing, Inc.

"Skip Weitzen does it again! *Hypergrowth* is amazing and will become required reading for those wanting to succeed in the white-knuckle decade of the 1990s. Why am I so sure of this? Because I bought 33,500 copies of Mr. Weitzen's last book and declared it 'must reading' for all of my business associates."

LANCE STRAUSS, President
Lance J. Strauss Enterprises, Inc.

"This book tells the story of hypergrowth previously untold . . . of performance, service, rapid development, and the creative use of information technology. As a chief executive officer of one of today's largest international humanitarian organizations, I found Skip Weitzen's insights to be refreshing, thorough, and applicable to the independent sector as well."

PAUL B. THOMPSON, Executive Director
World Vision Relief & Development Inc.

"When you read *Hypergrowth* you'll know why it's an anomaly. Weitzen speaks in the language that all of us must ultimately learn for our survival."

TONY BROWN
Tony Brown's Journal

"This book captures well the many things that companies have to do correctly and simultaneously to achieve hypergrowth. There are lessons for leaders of large businesses that need to boost growth as well as those small businesses that are destined to grow up quickly."

GEORGE S. SACERDOTE, Vice President
Arthur D. Little, Inc.

"Skip Weitzen clearly demonstrates that a critical condition underlying the success of hypergrowth companies is a value-added information management approach to every aspect of the business. Effective use of information technology is the glue that holds the hypergrowth company together through rapid marketplace changes."

DONALD A. MARCHAND, Dean, School of Information Studies
Syracuse University

"Mr. Weitzen has created a compelling cookbook for business success. He has shown us how companies break out of the intellectual confines of classical corporate culture to reap spectacular rewards. This is not a book for managers who are satisfied with conventional success. *Hypergrowth* is a "do-it-yourself" manual for those who dream of making a significant difference in the world of business. I recommend this book to anyone in corporate America who still has a shred of vision and initiative left in their soul."

MARSHALL TOPLANSKY, Chairman
Marketing Productivity Associates, Inc.

"Can you build a billion dollar business by reading *Hypergrowth?* Probably not, unless your timing is superb and you are above average in managerial ability. What Skip Weitzen clearly documents are the awesome opportunities in business today to achieve fame and fortune and a simple logical blueprint to reach your goals."

AL RIES, Chairman
Trout & Ries

"Skip Weitzen's examination of select, corporate success stories is not only a thorough analysis, but a how-to treatise on rapidly building an entrepreneurial company in the midst of changing business environments. From the standpoint of a business writer who covered Federal Express Corporation for four years, I believe Mr. Weitzen's prescription for hypergrowth is incisively on target. The flow charts he uses for each corporation also help illustrate the inner-workings that make these companies tick."

DAVID YAWN, Senior Staff Writer
Memphis Business Journal

"This book is an invaluable guide to the next generation of hypergrowth small business. Hopefully it will stimulate entrepreneurs and their investors to lead a new era of growth in America."

JERE W. GLOVER, Attorney & former officer
Small Business Administration

"*Hypergrowth* is TREMENDOUS! It's packed with challenging ideas and information. Skip Weitzen shows us that it can be done and how to do it."

CHARLES T. JONES, President
Life Management Services, Inc.

"*Hypergrowth* is not just another book about start-ups or 'excellent companies.' This compelling work provides the inspiration and the tools to reinvigorate any business, large or small, new or old."

GORDON F. MACPHERSON, JR., President
Incoming Calls Management Institute

HYPERGROWTH

Applying the Success Formula of
Today's Fastest Growing Companies

H. Skip Weitzen

John Wiley & Sons, Inc.
New York • Chichester • Brisbane • Toronto • Singapore

This book is dedicated to my children,
Jessica Grace
Cassandra Renee
Tiffany Joy
Rebekkah Leigh

In recognition of the importance of preserving what has been written, it is a policy of John Wiley & Sons, Inc., to have books of enduring value published in the United States printed on acid-free paper, and we exert our best efforts to that end.

This publication is designed to provide accurate and authoritative information in regard to the subject matter covered. It is sold with the understanding that the publisher is not engaged in rendering legal, accounting, or other professional services. If legal advice or other expert assistance is required, the services of a competent professional person should be sought. *From a Declaration of Principles jointly adopted by a Committee of the American Bar Association and a Committee of Publishers.*

Library of Congress Cataloging in Publication Data
Weitzen, H. Skip.
    Hypergrowth : applying the success formula of today's fastest growing companies / by H. Skip Weitzen.
        p.   cm.
    Includes index.
    ISBN 0-471-53173-1
    1. Industries, Size of—United States.   2. Big business-United States.   3. Organizational change—United States.   4. Success in business—United States.   I. Title.
HD69.S5W45   1991
658'.023—dc20   91-9619
                                                            CIP

Printed in the United States of America

10   9   8   7   6   5   4   3   2   1

Contents

Foreword

Many people point to the rapid change in technology in today's marketplace and marvel how we ever got along without personal computers, fax machines, VCR's and cellular phones. These things are very visible, very tangible, and have become a part of our everyday lives that did not exist just fifteen years ago. Less noticeable, but perhaps just as significant, the art and science of business management also has changed in the past fifteen years. In many ways, quite remarkably so.

I remember some of the lessons learned from the case study format when I was at Harvard Business School back in the early 1970s. Concepts such as incremental costing, break-even analysis and product/market segmentation were common. As a business consultant for McKinsey & Co. in the early 1980s I witnessed perhaps another new era; an era of empirically analyzing business successes and failures and the emergence of formulaic "business excellence" principles such as put forth in the best selling book, *In Search of Excellence.*

Today we may be witnessing yet another era with "borderless" companies and markets, global products and competition, totally new retailing formats and exotic new financing techniques. What sets the pace of these changes? How do the vanguard companies "discover" new competitive advantages to achieve superior market growth? In this most recent era, a diverse group of companies has shattered the old traditional principles of starting and running a business.

Skip Weitzen's book *Hypergrowth* is a ground-breaking study of these leading edge companies. For the first time it attempts

vii

to analyze and synthesize what sets these very different companies apart from the pack. I find the principles and examples as
relevant to the new entrepreneur as they are to Black &
Decker's quest for the next generation of major product innovations such as the Dustbuster or cordless power tools.

I have known Skip Weitzen for several years and have read his
previous books with interest and curiosity. Skip's way of drawing a thread through seemingly unrelated events to ascertain a
trend is quite unique and visionary. Even better for the reader,
his ability to reinforce rather innovative principles with enlight-
ening anecdotes is absorbing.

In addition to the "fun" of reading *Hypergrowth,* there are
many ways that budding entrepreneurs can get the most out of
this book. First, readers can use the principles to isolate their
own hypergrowth opportunities. It is an interesting exercise to
overlay the formulas onto your own current business plans.
Second, keep a copy of *Hypergrowth* near your desk or perhaps
on your nightstand for occasional reference and idea generation. You don't have to be an entrepreneur to apply some of the
lessons. There are many entrepreneurial opportunities even in
the largest business corporation for quick thinking managers.
Finally, *Hypergrowth* is required reading for anyone wanting to
improve their own track to business growth. Like the new art
student studying the masters, a lot can be learned by observing
the successes of our predecessors.

Gary T. DiCamillo
President, U.S. Power Tools
The Black & Decker Corporation

Preface

This book is about the 15 most dynamic companies in the history of commerce. Their pioneering achievements created a new business dynamic called *hypergrowth*. Removing all limits to growth, these companies provide hope for entrepreneurs, a structure for managers and clarity for executives.

These hypergrowth companies have one thing in common: they all went from start-up, relative dormancy, or standard growth into a hypergrowth pattern that was sustained for at least a decade under the same economic conditions. They all achieved the Fortune 500, then busted through the billion-dollar barrier . . . and lived to tell about it.

Hypergrowth is not unique to the go-go decade of the roaring '80s, since a new group of hypergrowth candidates has already emerged in the 1990s. With global production sources, sophisticated distribution infrastructures, and state-of-the-art information technologies all in place, fast growth companies are bursting through barrier after barrier in an entirely different economic environment. As you contemplate these corporate anomalies, remember that they are the growth models of the 21st century.

Acknowledgments

I want to acknowledge and thank the following people for their roles in this project:

- Maggie Moulton and Expectacion Rodriguez for their help in designing the operations overviews of America's fastest growing companies;
- Jim Williams, president of The Williams Inference Service, and David Jamison, editor of Anomaly Newsletter, whose work in the investment field provided the inspiration for The Hypergrowth Formula;
- Gwenyth Jones, my publisher at John Wiley & Sons, Inc., for helping structure a decade of research and thousands of pages notes;
- Readers of my previous books, *Infopreneurs: Turning Data into Dollars* and *Telephone Magic: How to Tap the Phone's Marketing Potential in Your Business* for telling me what you really wanted from a business book . . . I hope you enjoy reading this book as much as I enjoyed writing it; but remember that the most important part of this book is knowing how unimportant it is compared with knowing God. May He richly bless you.
- And finally, Julia, my *patient* and loving wife, for helping me pursue my dreams and visions.

Thank you.

I

The Hypergrowth Phenomenon

A successful executive visited his old business professor while attending a class reunion. He glanced down at the corrected exams on the professor's desk and exclaimed, "These exam questions are the same ones you gave us 25 years ago!" The professor calmly replied, "I know, I know. The questions are always the same, but today the answers are different."

HYPERGROWTH PIONEERS

During the decade of the 1980s, the following companies defined the new market phenomenon called Hypergrowth. These business anomalies of the 1980s are now the growth models for the 1990s:

Company: Business	Sales
Compaq: Computer Manufacturer	$0 to $2.9 billion
Businessland: Computer Retailer	$0 to $1.2 billion
Reebok: Shoe Manufacturer & Wholesaler	$1 million to $1.8 billion
Computer Associates: Computer Software Designer	$7 million to $1.1 billion
Seagate Technology: Computer Accessory Manufacturer	$10 million to $2.4 billion
Home Depot: Building Supply Retailer	$22 million to $2.8 billion
Liz Claiborne: Clothing Designer & Wholesaler	$79 million to $1.1 billion
Integrated Resources: Financial Services Company	$84 million to $1.7 billion
Apple Computer: Computer Manufacturer	$117 million to $5.3 billion
Tele-Communications, Inc.: Cable Television Company	$135 million to $3.0 billion
The Price Club: Membership Wholesaler	$146 million to $5.0 billion
MCI Communications: Telecommunications Company	$234 million to $6.5 billion
The Limited: Apparel Manufacturer & Retailer	$295 million to $4.6 billion
Federal Express: Air Freight Transportation Company	$415 million to $5.2 billion
Wal-Mart: Discount Merchandiser	$1.6 billion to $25.8 billion

1

The Dream Comes True

A handful of companies created today's "hypergrowth standard" when they each generated sales of one billion dollars or more within a decade of incorporating or emergence from relative dormancy.

The dream of amassing a great fortune quickly has been around since the beginning of commerce. However, the "hypergrowth phenomenon" began in 1982. That year, at age 6, Apple Computer became the youngest company to ever reach the Fortune 500—America's largest companies—producing the most remarkable growth pattern in business history.

Yet, entry to the Fortune 500 ($423 million in annual sales) is a long way from the billion-dollar plateau. Breaking through this billion-dollar barrier requires companies to shed their entrepreneurial shells, survive the bankers and lawyers, acclimate to the Fortune 500 pressures, develop new management teams, diversify product offerings, then expand globally. Amazingly, Apple accomplished all of this as it shattered the billion-dollar barrier just two years after reaching the Fortune 500 with revenues totaling $1.5 billion. Companies that experience hypergrowth—and continue to thrive—achieve the pinnacle of success in the world of business.

PLAN FOR HYPERGROWTH

Any company can experience hypergrowth, however, detailed planning prepares you for the hypergrowth rush and prevents your staff from becoming overwhelmed by its challenges. The following steps will help your hypergrowth dream become a reality:

Step 1: Ask the Right Questions

Hypergrowth results when you ask the right questions to eliminate the wrong answers and let the bad options fall away. Wrong answers to right questions can be remedied; but not asking the right questions can put you out of business. Some of these "right" questions include:

- What are your market's emerging needs?
- What products and services can be offered to meet these needs and create new business niches?
- What are the downside risks and upside potential of each opportunity?
- What resources are required to bring new products to market in half the time it currently takes?
- What new personnel will be required to manage your company as it enters into hypergrowth?

Step 2: Watch for Windows of Opportunity

All hypergrowth companies display an incredible sense of timing. With each company, a year in either direction at the start would have found their window of opportunity closed. Consider your hypergrowth window of opportunity:

- Where do you want to be 10 years from now?
- What is your compelling vision of the future?
- How will society be different in a decade?

- How will your market change during this period?
- What new products and emerging technologies will have the greatest impact on your market?

Step 3: Prepare Yourself for Growth

To prepare yourself for hypergrowth, become saturated with information about your industry, customers, competitors, products, distributors, and technologies. Then test your response to each hypergrowth opportunity by asking these key questions involving values:

- If money was not a problem and you knew you could not fail, what steps would you take today to seize a hypergrowth opportunity?
- Are you motivated more by money, recognition, or power?
- Can you stay focused on a single goal for a decade or more?
- Can your personal strengths be integrated with those of other associates to create a dynamic organization?
- Can you communicate your intentions verbally and in writing to garner the resources necessary to fuel hypergrowth?

INNOVATE THEN ACCELERATE

Hypergrowth is not another book about excellent companies. These are today's most dynamic enterprises—achieving incredible growth patterns for at least a decade to surpass $1 billion in sales.

Hypergrowth starts once *change* is considered the norm. Planning for change positions a company to ride its opportunities rather than react to them. Hypergrowth companies display speed and flexibility once they perceive or initiate change.

To experience hypergrowth, take great strides to nurture innovation. This starts with the search for niches and toeholds in the marketplace. Next, accelerate your operating pace. Speed will improve your company's strategic position and enhance your management effectiveness.

The key is to be different, then fast. Hypergrowth does not require wholly novel products. Some of the fastest growing companies simply provided innovative spins to existing products, then moved with alacrity to build sales, profits, and market share. The following companies created today's hypergrowth standard:

Compaq: From $0 to $2.9 Billion in Less Than a Decade

While Rod Canion of Compaq did not invent the computer, he introduced the first portable personal computer. Canion let his customers specify the computer functions, then his engineers designed them as small as possible. When Compaq committed to its first product, a 12-month development cycle was compressed into a 6-month adrenaline rush.

After Canion identified the costs associated with leaving a personal computer at the office, he manufactured his portable computer to outperform the industry standard. As a result, Compaq became the fastest growing start-up in business history—entering the Fortune 500 in its fourth year and surpassing the billion-dollar barrier a year later.

Businessland: From $0 to 1.2 Billion in Less Than a Decade

David Norman noticed that businesses were confused about how to integrate microcomputers into their mainframe environments. Norman believed that one day microcomputers would become a standard office tool. So he launched Businessland to support his local area network customers with implementation, consultation, documentation, training, and on-site services.

Norman's company became the leading value-added reseller with consistent products, pricing, service, and support. As a result, Businessland became the first company-owned microcomputer reseller to achieve revenues of $1 billion, after just eight years in business.

Reebok: From $1 Million to $1.8 Billion in a Decade

Paul Fireman uncovered new exercise niches to avoid head-on competition for his athletic shoes. After discovering the emerging aerobics niche, he quickly designed the first aerobics shoe for women. Once his Reebok footwear proved superior to the competition, Fireman moved fast to bring them to market.

Fireman helped millions of Americans participate in new athletic endeavors as he combined fashion and function into technologically superior footwear. As a result, Reebok grew from three hand-stitched shoe designs into 250 models in 12 categories. Fireman's shoes soon accounted for one-third of the 100 million pairs of athletic shoes annually sold in America.

Computer Associates: From $7 Million to $1.1 Billion in a Decade

Charles Wang designed innovative computer software when he discovered weaknesses in the software systems of America's biggest computer company—IBM. Computer Associates then acquired other software firms whose products could improve the performance of IBM's computers.

Wang figured that IBM would not sell software products that revealed its own problems. So his software marketing strategy became immune from the computer industry's most feared force. As a result, Computer Associates became the world's largest independent software company with more than 200 products designed for IBM mainframes.

Seagate Technology: From $10 Million to $2.4 Billion in a Decade

Alan Shugart applied innovation to the design, manufacturing, and marketing of high-quality data storage products. As a result, Seagate Technology captured nearly half of the global disk drive market after only seven years in business.

Although its key customers numbered fewer than 100, Seagate built and shipped more than 25 million disk drives during its hypergrowth decade. Alan Shugart offered original equipment manufacturers (OEMs) and other distributors the most diversified product line in the industry. The combination of manufacturing breakthroughs and efficient distribution systems gave Seagate industry dominance and the market low-cost disk drives.

Home Depot: From $22 Million to $2.8 Billion in a Decade

Bernard Marcus saw double-digit inflation and the do-it-yourself craze create the need for customer education in the building supply industry. So he trained Home Depot employees to educate do-it-yourself homeowners who lived in well-established transportation hubs.

Marcus offered his urban professional clientele extensive product training, quality service, and low prices. Equally important, he stocked everything needed to build and landscape an entire home from scratch. Home Depot became the prototype building supply chain that provided the next turn on the retail wheel.

Liz Claiborne: From $79 Million to $1.1 Billion in a Decade

Since innovation is a way of life in fashion design, Liz Claiborne broke the fashion year into six seasons. However, it was her speed and flexibility that allowed this fashion pioneer to deliver a new line of clothes every other month.

Avoiding the constraints of manufacturing facilities, Liz Claiborne met the needs of professional women for stylish and affordable clothing. Her innovative approach to design, production, and merchandising made this the first and only woman-led company to ever achieve $1 billion in sales from scratch.

Integrated Resources: From $84 Million to $1.7 Billion in a Decade

Selig Zises wanted to offer a different kind of investment service. So he created state-of-the-art tax shelter products.

Integrated Resources soon pioneered other innovative financial services that helped wealthy investors preserve their capital from taxes.

However, the government turned the tables on Zises with tax reforms. Integrated Resources quickly shifted its focus from shelters to insurance and became one of the world's largest financial services companies. Yet, spiraling debt and the lack of investor incentives caused the company to seek Chapter 11 bankruptcy protection after it topped $1 billion in sales.

Apple Computer: From $117 Million to $5.3 Billion in a Decade

Steve Jobs was a college drop-out who collected microprocessor parts. He built the first Apple Computer in his parents' garage. This product fueled the growth of the emerging personal computer market.

Apple Computer achieved critical mass by keeping its product lines simple, its marketing prominent, and its aftermarket focused on customer needs. Jobs sparked the Information Revolution as his company became the first personal computer manufacturing start-up to achieve the $1 billion sales plateau.

Tele-Communications, Inc.: From $135 Million to $3.0 Billion in a Decade

John Malone did not invent cable television. Instead, he purchased existing cable franchises to avoid new construction costs. Over a three-year period, Tele-Communications, Inc. (TCI) spent $3 billion and acquired 150 cable companies.

Malone's compelling vision of the future was that the country would someday be wired for cable television. So he created a major cable company that could compete with the networks for programming and advertising revenues. As a result of cable deregulation and aggressive acquisitions, TCI became America's largest cable enterprise.

The Price Club: From $146 Million to $5.0 Billion in a Decade

Sol Price was not the first businessman to keep his selling prices low. Yet offering only jumbo sizes, cases, cartons, and multiple-pack products helped The Price Club achieve the highest sales volumes and the fastest inventory turns ever witnessed by the retail or discount industries.

Sol and his son Robert observed that most distributors wouldn't stop at a business for less than $500 in sales. So they designed a new distribution channel to sell top-of-the-line merchandise at margins less than 10 percent over manufacturing cost. As a result, The Price Club achieved complete inventory turnover every 16 days and spawned the multi-billion dollar warehouse club industry.

MCI Communications Corporation: From $234 Million to $6.5 Billion in a Decade

William McGowan believed that with AT&T owning 100 percent of the long distance market, they had nowhere to go but down. He was convinced that competition in the long distance telephone market would improve service and lower prices. So McGowan spent millions of dollars in legal fees to open up the long distance market for his fledgling company, MCI.

After single-handedly dismantling the telephone monopoly, McGowan quickly invested billions of dollars to build MCI its own telecommunications network. Soon after, this small microwave communications enterprise grew into America's second largest long distance company.

The Limited: From $295 Million to $4.6 Billion in a Decade

Leslie Wexner made extraordinary efforts to meet the quality and fashion demands of his budget customers. He shadowed emerging sportswear trends and sold low-priced look-alikes exclusively through a galaxy of The Limited stores.

Wexner's trendy fashions were at the heart of his revolutionary mass merchandising formula. Through overseas manufacturing and integrated distribution, The Limited became the fastest growing, most profitable specialty retailer in the world.

Federal Express: From $415 Million to $5.2 Billion in a Decade

Fred Smith did not invent air cargo delivery. Instead, he created hub-and-spoke delivery for time-definite, high priority packages. Convinced that passenger route systems were wrong for freight distribution, Smith launched Federal Express when he was only 27.

While on the verge of bankruptcy, Smith raised more than $50 million from investors and got Congress to remove its air cargo restrictions. This allowed Smith to pioneer an industry that became the logistics arm for the service economy. Within its decade of hypergrowth, Federal Express made instant gratification an ingrained part of American culture.

Wal-Mart: From $1.6 Billion to $25.8 Billion in a Decade

Sam Walton provided the standard for innovation in the general merchandise retailing industry. His Wal-Mart empire focused on the needs of downscale consumers who buy billions of dollars of basic merchandise each year.

Wal-Mart offered one-stop family shopping for a wide variety of products at everyday low prices. Once his concept caught on, Walton created 254,000 new jobs in his hypergrowth decade— more than any other American company during that same period and amassed a personal fortune surpassing $6 billion.

REWRITE THE RULES

Hypergrowth expresses itself in ways unfamiliar to traditional schools of thought. You will rewrite the rules of business as you create manufacturing miracles, productivity breakthroughs, and distribution revolutions. The key to your hypergrowth is to innovate, then accelerate. Remember, you don't always have to be first, but you've got to be fast.

WITH HYPERGROWTH, EVERYBODY WINS!

Hypergrowth is a vital business dynamic. It reflects a radically changing marketplace as hypergrowth companies redefine the rules of commerce. The benefits of their accomplishments are shared by corporations, consumers, and communities around the world.

Advantages for Other Corporations

Besides the benefits accrued by the hypergrowth companies, other corporations benefit from the hypergrowth phenomenon as they learn:

- Ways to spot hypergrowth opportunities before they emerge
- Secrets to making the most of a market niche
- Innovative ways to fund fast growth
- Creative management techniques
- Ways to gain a competitive edge from distribution
- Simple strategies that extend growth curves
- Methods for attracting top quality personnel.

Consumer Advantages

Hypergrowth is the tangible expression of the fundamental free market value "find a need and fill it." Companies that grow quickly give consumers what they want, when they want it, at a fair price. Consumers are the ultimate beneficiaries as they get:

- Innovative and superior products
- Convenient locations and extended hours of operation
- Better product selections at lower prices
- Worry-free shopping with money-back guarantees
- Around-the-clock product information and service

Community Advantages

Hypergrowth companies typically establish overseas manufacturing sites to take advantage of cheap natural resources and vast labor pools. Benefits flow to both the local and international communities as hypergrowth offers:

- New jobs and new labor skills
- Improved standards of living
- New uses of a community's resources
- Access to import and export pools
- New production and communications opportunities.

Create the New Business Model

Hypergrowth is an anomaly that baffles most experts. However, its amazing benefits have transformed the business anomaly into a state-of-the-art business model.

Hypergrowth's impact can dictate what you will produce, where you will work, and how you will transact business. This phenomenon will also produce significant shifts in key economic factors such as growth, productivity, earnings, return on investment, employment, consumption, and international trade.

Achieving the hypergrowth standard set by these companies is not the final criterion for success; committing to pursue hypergrowth means you are already a success.

2

The Hypergrowth Formula

Hypergrowth is the process of capitalizing an above average rate of return for a decade or more. It combines two concepts, *hyper* (in abnormal excess) and *growth* (increase in size, number, and value) to produce this new market phenomenon.

Hypergrowth begins with the search for early signs of change. Sometimes the market initiates that change and creates the demand for new products. At other times, the product drives the change in market behavior. In both cases, hypergrowth companies transform themselves quickly from entrepreneurial phenoms into mature market leaders.

Hypergrowth results when you establish, then pursue, the highest conceptual model of change. The better your model, the more directed your activities, the more likely you will achieve hypergrowth. Next, simplify your model into a business formula.

For example, the hypergrowth formula (Figure 2.1) begins with a thorough understanding of existing business and industry norms. Any activity that does not conform to these norms is called an *anomaly*. Next, a *metonymy* shows the impact of an anomaly on business or industry. The *inference* is the interpretation of the anomalous activity that confirms an emerging order. Market *penetration* through new products and enhanced services either creates a short-lived fad or a new market *trend*. Finally, *hypergrowth* slows as trends mature.

15

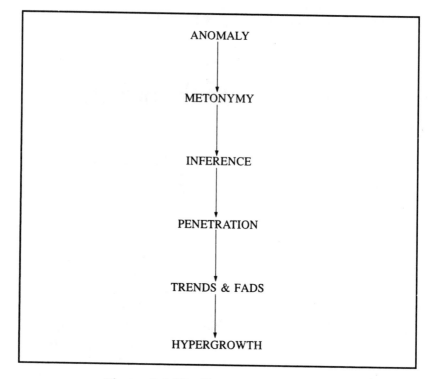

Figure 2.1 The Hypergrowth Formula

ANOMALY: FOR THE FIRST TIME

Any new activity that creates a gap between an actual and a perceived reality is known as an anomaly. Since anomalies always surround newness, these incongruous aberrations provide clues to hidden change and potential hypergrowth opportunities.

As early indicators of change, anomalies challenge the status quo. They initiate a new order with the potential for capitalizing an above average rate of return in a short period of time.

METONYMY: THE EMERGING ORDER

A metonymy depicts the businesses and industries affected as an anomaly impacts the status quo. It is the context in which you would be operating. When the anomaly portends significant change, the metonymy clarifies who will benefit from the emerging order.

Change becomes particularly meaningful when the parts (anomalies) are linked to the whole (metonymy). Flexible entrepreneurs are often closest to those markets bristling with abnormalities, aberrations, and anomalies. So they, rather than the entrenched Fortune 500, are first to respond with new offerings from emerging industries.

INFERENCE: OPPORTUNITIES AND RISKS

Inference is a conclusion based on a premise that links cause and effect. Inference is a lot like going fishing . . . when you feel a nibble on the line, it is time to reel the fish in. With inference, your hunch means it is time to start piecing together the hypergrowth puzzle.

The inference, formed through inductive reasoning, is actually based on the relationship of the anomaly to the metonymy. To confirm an inference's accuracy, be sure to find several observations that lead to the same conclusion.

PENETRATION: REACHING THE TRENDSETTERS

Next, establish practical steps to reach those trendsetters who spark hypergrowth. Constant exposure to your product among those who influence brand preference can stimulate fast growth.

Generally, trendsetters provide the leading indicator of product preference. Once your product is in their hands, reinforce their buying decisions through word-of-mouth advertising and targeted media support. Finally, roll out other products and services through predetermined distribution channels.

TRENDS AND FADS: HYPERGROWTH SLOWS AS TRENDS MATURE

New business opportunities or shifts in consumer behavior are the forces that create fads (short-lived patterns) and trends (new market directions). Hypergrowth results from associating your products with these forces early in the growth cycle . . . like a surfer catching a giant wave at its formation.

Hypergrowth companies stay ahead of the economic, social, political, and technological shifts that force rapid changes upon their industries. So continually seek out new anomalies since hypergrowth slows as trends mature.

WHAT TO DO ONCE YOU SPOT AN ANOMALY

The hypergrowth formula can help you identify emerging billion-dollar opportunities. After spotting an anomaly, gather more background information on the change. Then overlay its metonymy to depict those companies impacted by the anomaly. Next, infer the possible consequences and classify your inferences into known (in the public domain) or unknown (hidden or purposely concealed) opportunities.

Sorting out anomalies is a critical first step. When anomalies emerge within rapidly changing social and business norms, they reveal impending change. As these unique events cluster, the emerging order creates pockets of hypergrowth.

Hypergrowth requires that you act prematurely on an inner hunch. More often than not, your hunch will be based on a partial picture of the opportunity. However, when your activities are directed by the highest conceptual model of change, your hypergrowth opportunity will become easier to see.

The hypergrowth formula can be overlayed onto America's fastest growing companies to help you understand this new phenomenon.

Example 1

The hypergrowth formula explains why Compaq became America's fastest growing start-up, maturing into a $2.9 billion superstar just eight years after incorporating:

Anomaly   Hypergrowth begins when you spot an early sign of change. Either the market initiates this change and creates a demand for new products or a new product drives the market change. In the case of Compaq, its computer was the first portable version of IBM's personal computer. Portability was an anomaly that heralded fundamental changes in the marketplace.

Metonymy   The metonymy depicts businesses and industries impacted by the anomaly. Rod Canion calculated that the productivity gains from taking a personal computer home after work were significant enough to account for a new industry niche.

Inference   The inference is a conclusion based on a premise that links a cause and effect. Rod Canion inferred that software writers would not design programs for unknown computers. So he committed from the start to making his Compaq portable computer IBM-compatible.

Penetration   Compaq needed to penetrate the dealer network to make its product launch a success and to force open the gap that portability created. Rod Canion lured away the sales manager from IBM's PC team to guarantee that Compaq would get its share of shelf space coming out of the blocks.

Trend   Compaq created a new market direction when it took business computing power from the office and gave it portability. Rod Canion helped usher in a new generation of the personal computer revolution as microcomputer sales soon outpaced revenues of mainframes and minis . . . from a market that didn't even exist a decade earlier.

Hypergrowth　Compaq capitalized an above average rate of return in a short period of time. As a result, it became the world's leading manufacturer of portable personal computers with 3,000 authorized dealers in 40 countries.

Example 2

By applying the hypergrowth formula you'll see how MCI emerged from relative obscurity to become America's second leading long distance company with sales surpassing $6.5 billion:

Anomaly　When Bill McGowan visited the public reading room of the Federal Communications Commission (FCC), he uncovered an anomaly: AT&T had never been granted a legal monopoly for long distance communications. Realizing that AT&T simply evolved into its monopoly erased the gap between McGowan's perceived and actual realities.

Metonymy　Armed with the knowledge that he could short-circuit AT&T's claim to a long distance monopoly, McGowan viewed microwave communications as an inexpensive way to transmit telephone calls. Bypassing the telephone cable infrastructure would certainly challenge Ma Bell's hold on long distance calling.

Inference　Bill McGowan inferred that he could build a big company by offering AT&T's business customers discounted long distance service. After all, AT&T's disproportionate business prices helped subsidize residential telephone service.

Penetration　With $115 million raised from investors, Bill McGowan constructed microwave transmission towers for specialized long distance service. He then relocated MCI's headquarters in Washington, DC, and began to penetrate the federal regulatory agencies with his antitrust lawsuits.

Trend The FCC granted MCI a green light to operate under the terms of a "modular tariff." MCI then expanded its toehold into discounted services for millions of AT&T customers. This was the start of the long distance pricing wars.

Hypergrowth MCI won its antitrust case against AT&T, which led to deregulated telephone service and the rush of new activity known as hypergrowth.

HOW TO APPLY THE HYPERGROWTH FORMULA

Anomalies in the corporate setting are often dismissed because managers focus on efficiency—doing things right. Hypergrowth companies, however, seize anomalies as they focus on effectiveness—doing the right things. Anomalies are the starting point for hypergrowth since they reveal the first signs of change in the marketplace.

Newspapers and trade publications report anomalies because they are newsworthy. Key words and phrases that point out these early signs of change include:

"For the first time . . ."

"In an unusual turn of events . . ."

"All of a sudden . . ."

"In an unprecedented move . . ."

"The unique product . . ."

When a shift in market behavior is reported, stay focused on the anomaly. Then place the anomaly into its metonymy and infer the impact on your business.

You have seen how Compaq and MCI applied the hypergrowth formula to achieve their success. Now let's apply the same formula to some current anomalies that display the earmarks of hypergrowth. Overlaying the hypergrowth formula onto these anomalies gives you a chance to create your own hypergrowth opportunity:

Opportunity 1: Superconductors

Anomaly   In a recent breakthrough, superconductors transmitted data at 100 times the speed of fiber optic networks.

Metonymy   Data activity has surpassed voice traffic over fiber optic networks.

Inference   Since fiber optic networks replaced copper phone lines due to productivity breakthroughs, superconductors will most likely replace fiber optic networks for the same reason.

Penetration   Determine which raw materials are used in superconducting communications networks and become a player in the manufacturing and distribution of its components.

Trend   Superconductors will usher in a global economy with instant communications.

Opportunity 2: Solar Energy

Anomaly   An experimental solar collector recently generated 84,000 times the sun's normal intensity level on earth. This device concentrated sunlight to an intensity 15 percent greater than on the surface of the sun itself.

Metonymy   The cost to produce a watt of energy with photovoltaics is now the most competitive among energy production methods.

Inference   As oil spills and nuclear accidents create regional disasters, solar becomes the environmentalists' energy of choice.

Penetration List the major consumer applications of photo-voltaic technology and establish a wholesale distribution channel to service these specific market niches.

Trend Solar energy will be a major player in the "Save the Earth" movement.

Opportunity 3: Manufacturing

Anomaly A French garment factory started to mass produce custom design suits at one-half the price of American tailors with a telephone/satellite/computer hook-up.

Metonymy Foreign manufacturers now integrate telecommunications with manufacturing to gain instant access to the American marketplace.

Inference The local market favors overseas production of customized goods due to the low cost of labor.

Penetration Establish a telecommunications link to deliver local markets to custom manufacturers.

Trend Shopping for customized products from global sources will become as easy as buying from a mail order catalog.

Opportunity 4: Senior Citizens

Anomaly *Modern Maturity* just became the largest circulation magazine in America.

Metonymy A major focus of the seniors market centers around cost-effective quality health care.

Inference Outpatient services that target the elderly will continue to thrive as the aging population bulges.

Penetration   Gather catalogs of all medical, communications, and health-related products utilized by hospice services and become a value-added reseller.

Trend   The mobile, independent elderly market is one of the fastest growing sectors of society, preferring outpatient care from their homes over expensive hospital stays.

Opportunity 5: Communications

Anomaly   For the first time, Chrysler's annual shareholder meeting was carried over the caller-pays 900-number telephone network for those who could not attend in person.

Metonymy   The emerging infotext industry has grown from start-up to $3 billion in revenues in just three years.

Inference   Companies will disseminate their information over 900 numbers to reduce costs, increase productivity, and generate revenue.

Penetration   Align with long distance phone companies, equipment manufacturers, local exchange carriers, and audio-text service bureaus to spur interactive applications of 900-number technology.

Trend   Small companies will achieve around-the-clock, nationwide market coverage at a profit as 900 numbers replace toll-free calls.

PLAN YOUR WORK, THEN WORK YOUR PLAN

When you overlay the hypergrowth formula onto your current business plan, you can uncover new market opportunities. These may first appear as anomalies or aberrations. Don't

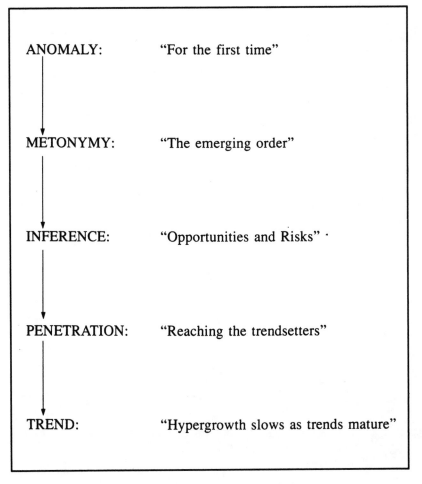

ANOMALY: "For the first time"

METONYMY: "The emerging order"

INFERENCE: "Opportunities and Risks" ·

PENETRATION: "Reaching the trendsetters"

TREND: "Hypergrowth slows as trends mature"

Figure 2.2 Hypergrowth Worksheet

dismiss them. Instead observe where the anomalies tend to cluster.

Next, use the hypergrowth worksheet (Figure 2.2) to test the validity of every anomaly you encounter. Analyze the metonymy to determine if the emerging order could have significant impact on your current business. If it does, nurture the anomaly, since it represents your hypergrowth opportunity.

3

Hypergrowth Pressure Points

I n the hypergrowth formula, the first step is to isolate anomalies that emerge at pressure points and lead to pattern breaks in the market. This process of qualifying anomalies screens out those that are interesting—even fascinating, but that don't portend enormous growth possibilities. Once you are certain that an anomaly has emerged at a pressure point, position your product or service so the rush of hypergrowth activity can occur.

A superior knowledge of the marketplace is the starting point for recognizing a pressure point and the potential for hypergrowth. An intimate awareness of business dynamics and consumer behavior helps identify emerging incongruities.

Tracking the anomaly to its pressure point helps identify the origination of the hypergrowth opportunity. Remember, immediate response to an anomaly at its pressure point with a well-positioned product or service is the hallmark of successful hypergrowth companies.

HOW TO LOCATE A PRESSURE POINT

To initiate the hypergrowth process, you must observe an anomaly at its pressure point. Pressure points are nearly impossible to quantify early on. Analysts typically miss anomalies and pressure points and their subsequent capitalization opportunities because they demand quantification before acknowledging the change. However, documented change generally means that a pressure point and its anomaly have matured and the corresponding hypergrowth window has closed.

Pressure points can be identified through a seven-step process that is easy to integrate into your current business environment.

Step 1: Challenge Your Assumptions

Everybody makes assumptions about their world of business. Allow anomalies to challenge your business philosophies so when the market shifts, your operating assumptions can shift with it.

Step 2: Look for Changing Patterns

Identify pressure points by searching for new activities that might impact your business. Establish an intimate awareness of your marketplace by reading trade, technical, and consumer publications.

Step 3: Create an Anomaly Sieve

Pressure points can be isolated as anomalies pass through a sieve that retains all information that is new or unexpected and discards all other input that is expected, extraneous, repetitive, irrelevant, or routine. Set up a filing system to store, monitor, and update anomalies at their emerging pressure points.

Step 4: Verify Relevant Pressure Points

Once you observe the anomaly of a pressure point, verify its cause and effect. Consider every possible hypergrowth scenario and rank them based on their potential returns.

Step 5: Establish a Course of Action

It is unrealistic to plan strategies for anomalies that have yet to occur. Plan your course of action based on current anomalies and pressure points, rather than on past assumptions tied to future hopes.

Step 6: Accelerate Your Adaptation

Once an anomaly and its pressure point have been detected, accelerate your adaptation to that change. By the time the numbers accrue, the hypergrowth opportunity will be obvious to most observers, including your competition.

Step 7: Minimize Your Risks

Fine tune your internal strategy before announcing your plans to the public. This will place your company on the road to hypergrowth and make it nearly impossible for the competition to catch up.

COMMON HYPERGROWTH PRESSURE POINTS

Anomalies that erupt at pressure points don't have to be revolutionary to result in hypergrowth. Often just minor adjustments in product design or a slight shift in the environment creates the hypergrowth rush. Anomalies that lead to hypergrowth typically emerge among the following pressure points.

Pressure Point 1: Market Niches

The mass market has been segmented so that hypergrowth typically emerges from tiny niches. To initiate hypergrowth, carve out a business niche, build market share, then expand your market. If you don't think it's a niche environment, then try allocating your national advertising campaign budget: TV (4,200 cable systems, some with more than 100 channels); radio (8,500 stations with 158 different music formats); direct mail (nearly 100,000 mailing lists available for rent). The tiny athletic shoe segment is an example of this niche environment. It grew to become one of the largest producers of the entire shoe industry.

Reebok became the largest maker of athletic footwear by recognizing hot athletic niches, such as aerobics, tennis, and walking, then becoming synonymous with those niches through its products. Observing trend-setting Southern Californians at health clubs and social gatherings helped Reebok jump on new athletic activities with unique shoe designs.

Paul Fireman obtained the North American rights to a small line of running shoe he saw at a trade show. Named for an African gazelle, Reebok began manufacturing shoes in 1895 from a depressed area of Bolton, England. The unique track shoe was immortalized in the movie, *Chariots of Fire,* the story of Britain's 1924 Olympic track team.

After just two years, Fireman went broke promoting the market's most expensive shoe to a largely indifferent audience. Fireman negotiated for and received a $77,500 cash infusion from British shoe distributor, Pentland Industries plc, in exchange for 56 percent ownership in Reebok North America.

With some breathing room, Paul Fireman looked for new exercise niches to avoid head-on competition with industry leader Nike. After discovering aerobics, Fireman manufactured the first aerobics shoe designed for women. The "Freestyle," a terry-cloth-lined sneaker, resembled a jazz shoe. Its radical departure in technology offered special support features that minimized shin splints.

Fireman worked hard to solidify a leadership role for Reebok within the emerging aerobics niche. He underwrote the first studies in aerobic-related injuries and sponsored a certification program for aerobics instructors. Then, he built a nationwide affiliation with aerobics leaders through Reebok's Professional Instructor Alliance.

When Paul Fireman took Reebok public, the stock opened at $17, rose to $83 then split three for one within its first year. Over its hypergrowth decade, Reebok's revenues soared from

$1 million to $1.9 billion as it grew from three hand-stitched shoe designs to 250 models in 12 categories.

Flush with cash, Paul Fireman went on an acquisitions binge. He acquired control of Reebok from the Foster family for just $700,000. Within a 14-month period, Reebok's five main operating units came to include Reebok North America (Reebok Footware, Reebok Apparel, Metaphors, and Reebok Canada), Reebok International (worldwide marketer of Reebok), Rockport (walking shoes), Avia (performance athletic shoes), and Ellese (Italian sportswear and athletic shoe company).

Exploiting new athletic niches at their inception accounts for Reebok's meteoric rise. While most athletic shoe companies were focused on running, the oldest manufacturer of running shoes fueled the aerobics and fitness trends. Paul Fireman's design innovations and new shoe categories tied neatly into his market niches and catapulted Reebok to the top of the athletic shoe market.

Pressure Point 2: Product Standards

When a product provides customers with the most quality and best value, it takes its place as the standard in the market. Product standards are established by market leaders as quality and value differentiate them from the competition. Market share and profits quickly follow. To achieve the product standard in your industry, acquire an intimate knowledge of the product leader and the end-user consumer. Then offer products that provide the best in value, durability, and productivity.

Compaq's initial strategy was to build computers that outperformed the computer industry standard. As Rod Canion designed innovative features, higher quality, and greater value into his products, Compaq soon became the world's leading manufacturer of personal computers. Compaq, in fact, became the only personal computer company to establish a better quality brand name than IBM.

For 13 years, Rod Canion had tolerated corporate bureaucracy at Texas Instruments. The turning point came when he was assigned to create TI's office microcomputer. Canion understood the role of IBM's personal computer and its position in the marketplace. He finally resigned because TI's management would not acknowledge the importance of IBM's product standard.

Canion and two associates started Gateway Technology. Their plan called for circuit cards to expand the storage capacity of IBM Personal Computers. Sent back to the drawing board by venture capitalists, Rod Canion sketched his new idea on a restaurant napkin: A portable version of IBM's Personal Computer. The idea clicked and the company changed its name to Compaq.

Canion decided his computer needed to be IBM-compatible since software writers would not design programs for unknown computers. So Compaq became the first computer to share the fast-growing library of IBM PC software.

Compaq started on the proverbial shoestring. The Sevin Rosen Management Company put up $20,000 for Canion to develop a prototype. A fresh $1.5 million in seed money let Canion and his team manufacture the first portable computer. It weighed 28 pounds, had a 9-inch screen, and retailed for $2,995.

Rod Canion then secured $30 million more in venture capital to expand production capacity 100-fold and increase employment from 3 to 450. Several months later, Canion raised another $66 million in a public offering that fueled $111 million in first year sales. It was the most successful start-up in American business history. IBM soon responded with its own portable computer. Yet Compaq outsold IBM's portable 5-to-1 as its revenues tripled to $329 million. The next year, Compaq doubled its lead over IBM's portable. Then, just four years after incorporation, Compaq became the youngest company ever to join the prestigious Fortune 500.

In its fifth year of operation, Compaq sales surpassed one billion dollars, faster than any other U.S. manufacturer. Even more remarkable, Compaq's birth and hypergrowth occurred during an industry-wide sales slump. Compaq's hypergrowth reflected its ability to understand and meet its customers' needs for increased productivity. Improving upon the industry standard helped Compaq achieve the highest new product success rate in the computer industry.

Pressure Point 3: Inflationary Markets

A rapid price increase that tends to distort income distribution is called inflation. While mild inflation is an annoyance if accompanied by full employment, at its worse, inflation invites panic buying and a possible collapse of the monetary system. Excess demand and high costs push and pull an economy into inflation. Like a wire hanger that you bend back and forth, when the push and pull of inflation heats up the economy, it can snap.

The do-it-yourself craze emerged amidst double-digit inflation, rising construction costs and record-high mortgage rates. Bernard Marcus started Home Depot to help do-it-yourselfers fight inflation. Marcus created a retailing revolution when he realized that three out of four homeowners complete at least one fix-it project on their residence each year.

Do-it-yourselfers (DIY) soon emerged as one of America's most powerful buying forces—driving the $100 billion-a-year home improvement industry. Home Depot actually helped DIYers save up to 60 percent of a project's cost by showing them how to do the work themselves.

Marcus was acutely aware of inflation and its impact on his market. He watched the do-it-yourself market become flooded with how-to-books, video tapes, magazines, television shows, workshops, and training schools.

Marcus designed his store to ride the crest of this DIY craze and help take the sting out of inflation. He piled inventory high into the aisles. He created Home Depot's 40-page "catabooks" to promote items sold at discount prices. Home Depot executives participated in call-in radio program that gave do-it-yourselfers answers to their home improvement questions.

Hard-nosed buying and sharp-eyed selling typify the Home Depot warehouse retailing style. However, Home Depot's unusually helpful customer service differentiates it from the competition. Home Depot employs 90 percent of its staff on a full-time basis. With higher salaries and full benefits, employees deliver the best customer service in the industry.

To open a new Home Depot store costs $8 million. Land and building shell costs $4 million while inventory of 25,000 different items accounts for the balance. During its hypergrowth, Home Depot placed stores across the southern half of the United States. Store sizes varied, with the largest consisting of 140,000 square feet plus an outdoor selling area for landscaping supplies.

Just over a decade after he was fired from his job as a Handy Dan store manager, Bernard Marcus generated sales of $2.8 billion from his 118 Home Depot stores. When Bernard Marcus discovered that inflation created a hypergrowth pressure point, he created a way for American consumers to increase the value of a treasured investment—their homes.

Pressure Point 4: Business Flaws

Business flaws can reveal pressure points that lead to hypergrowth. Identify these flaws by listening for the root causes of customer complaints. Jot down what you hear. Then look for an angle, a concept, a strategy, or a tactic that can mend the flaw in the marketplace. More often than not, the corresponding solution to the business flaw does not look too exciting. However, once your business strategy unleashes its hypergrowth rush, you'll be happy with the results.

The warehouse outlet concept, for instance, emerged from Sol Price's perception that small businesses lacked an efficient wholesaler. The Price Club became the first discount retailer to exploit flaws in the wholesale distribution system. As a result, it muscled in on the once exclusive domain of supermarkets, catalog stores, and discounters.

Sol and his son Robert raised $2.5 million and opened the first Price Club in a former aircraft parts factory in San Diego. As president and chief executive officer, Robert ran the day-to-day operations. This freed Chairman Sol to conjure up new ideas and business formulas.

The no-frills cash-and-carry Price Club offered merchandise from among just 4,000 stock-keeping units. Its small assortment of goods also came in the largest sizes and in limited brands. To garner the highest possible share of a group member's family spending, Price Club's product mix was well planned: sundries, 30 percent; food, 26 percent; appliances and housewares, 20 percent; hardlines, 12 percent; soft goods, 7 percent; and liquor, 5 percent. The Price Club's minimal gross margin strategy helped maximize sales and accelerate inventory turnover.

While the off-price apparel industry was an extension of apparel retailing, Price Club warehousing emerged as an entirely new business concept. It was based as much on logistics and cost savings as on merchandising. Robert Price limited his inventory selection and the availability of membership privileges. These stringent policies attracted the highest average membership income in the industry at $32,000 per year.

Its steep barrier to entry included land, buildings, and fixtures, which run $5 million per facility. An inventory investment of $2 million is required until sales exceed 15 turns per year. Indeed, the very concept of operating at gross margins of under 10 percent discouraged most traditional retailers from entering the industry.

Numbers hardly tell the whole story, but they are a good indicator of The Price Club's staggering success in exploiting a business flaw. It became one of the greatest retailing success stories as a $5,000 investment in The Price Club start-up was worth $2.5 million a decade later.

Pressure Point 5: Customer Needs

Hypergrowth results when you give enough customers what they want, when they want it, where they want it, at fair prices. To get what you ultimately want, you must put your customers' needs slightly ahead of your own personal agenda. In business this is known as "find a need and fill it." Unless your market research identifies such fundamental market needs, you are wasting your R&D dollars.

Liz Claiborne, for example, started her company based on the observation that working women lacked stylish clothes. Claiborne became the first fashion designer to recognize and capitalize on the needs of the emerging American business-woman. As professional women focused on dressing for suc-cess, Claiborne designed stylish clothes to fit their budgets.

At age 47, with $75,000 in life savings and $180,000 from family and friends, she launched Liz Claiborne, Inc. Her dreams were to design clothes for professional women, get her name on the label and build a small business. Instead she created a fashion empire that steered women from blue-suit uniforms into comfortable, colorful clothes. Claiborne transcended her dreams by becoming a woman-led global enterprise.

Liz Claiborne isolated an anomaly at its related pressure point: The influx of 48 million American businesswomen spawned new dress and accessory demands. Claiborne was there to meet the needs of the fashion-conscious professional.

The majority of these working women did not require formal executive wear so they dressed casually. Claiborne designed for them affordable wardrobes with depth and versatility. These same working women also needed weekend wear that suited their lifestyles. So she created sportswear lines with a casual look. When consumer acceptance came, cosmetics and acces-sories followed.

One of Claiborne's supreme innovations was to break the fashion year into six seasons. She added extra spring and fall lines that met consumers' needs for fresh fashion designs. This also committed Claiborne to creating a new line of clothes every eight weeks.

Another Claiborne breakthrough was to operate without a road salesforce. The point of contact for her thousands of retailers became face-to-face meetings at Claiborne's New York showroom. Liz used this forum to carefully focus on the needs of her 100 largest clients who generated 75 percent of Claiborne sales.

Liz Claiborne understood the needs of her customers. She carefully studied their lifestyles and knew the prices they would pay for clothes. By meeting her customers' needs, Liz

Claiborne became the first and only woman-led company ever to generate annual sales in excess of one billion dollars.

Pressure Point 6: Legislative Changes

Legislative changes represent a powerful pressure point. Government can be your biggest ally or foe—depending on which side of the legislation you sit. Its decisions and regulations shape corporate America. Companies that achieve hypergrowth as a result of the legislative process, are well-versed in how bills become laws, how to register lobbyists, and how to form a political action committee.

Tele-Communications, Inc. (TCI), for example, was an early participant in the cable television industry. It spent nearly two decades in relative dormancy. When Congress deregulated cable, TCI entered into hypergrowth. Free to expand, TCI acquired so many cable systems it achieved near-monopoly status.

It wasn't always easy for John Malone. TCI was constantly fighting with bankers and cable regulators just to survive. After four years with Malone at the helm, TCI generated its first significant cash flow. Malone then convinced a group of institutional lenders to front TCI $77 million, the largest cable TV loan ever. The cash infusion launched TCI's cable acquisition strategy. John Malone started purchasing existing cable franchises rather than take on new cable construction costs. Although TCI assumed heavy debt, it also generated phenomenal cash flow as the cable industry flourished.

Following deregulation, John Malone steered clear of bidding wars unless a big-city cable operator could not fulfill its extravagant promises. Malone, for example, acquired the Pittsburgh franchise after it lost nearly $30 million. He dismantled the expensive interactive system and offered subscribers barebones cable service. The franchise turned around and produced a million dollars a month in cash flow for TCI.

John Malone helped TCI achieve hypergrowth because he was in the right place to take advantage of new legislation. Although broadcasters decide what programs to offer, John Malone decides whether or not to broadcast them. That makes him a formidible gatekeeper to millions of cable homes. The combination of deregulation and hard-nosed management turned a financially strapped rural cable company into an entertainment force that rivaled the television networks and the movie studios.

Pressure Point 7: Competitive Strategies

Marketing not only involves satisfying customer needs, it takes into account competitive strategies. Knowing your company's position relative to the competition can reveal anomalies at a pressure point. Understand how your competitors identify customer needs, conceptualize products, manufacture and distribute these products, communicate their offerings and fulfill their promises. Once you identify the weak points of a competitor's strategies, attack hard with creative products and marketing campaigns. This is exactly how Wal-Mart entered into hypergrowth.

Sam Walton saw major changes on the horizon as his variety stores started losing market share to emerging discounters, most notably, Kmart. While many executives scoffed at Walton's desire to enter the new discount business, Walton simply responded to his competitive threats by opening his own discount stores. Walton learned everything he could about discounting by hiring away the best people from his most successful competitors.

Walton's small town discount stores offered friendly service, name-brand merchandise, and low prices. With his operating system refined, Walton proceeded to open 18 Wal-Mart stores in four states. A decade later, 276 Wal-Mart stores served rural populations ranging from 5,000 to 25,000. Wal-Mart sales soared from $44 million to $1.6 billion.

Sam Walton then focused on Wal-Mart's hypergrowth expansion. In its hypergrowth decade, Wal-Mart placed more than 1,500 stores in 25 states. Walton then diversified with Sam's Wholesale Clubs, **dot** Discount Drug Stores, Helen's Arts and Crafts Stores, and Hypermart*USA. Sam's generated profits on high volume turnover and low margins; **dot** drew on Wal-Mart's experience in mass distribution of merchandise; Helen's tested a specialty merchandise niche, but later closed down; Hypermart*USA, Walton's 200,000-square-foot "mall without walls," combined grocery, general merchandise, fast food, and service stores to create a one-stop shopping experience. Wal-Mart sales burgeoned from $1.6 billion to $25.8 billion.

Wal-Mart's expansion program, two store openings a week, generated sales growth at three times the average rate for the discount store industry. Its no-frills atmosphere appealed to a predominantly blue-collar clientele. Yet, Walton differentiated his discount stores from the competition with inspired employees who all carry the title of "associate," and brand-name merchandise.

Wal-Mart adapted to competitive pressures from Kmart and other discounters to change the American retail scene. Wal-Mart produced the highest return on equity among retailers and the greatest margins of all variety stores. At 69 years of age, Sam Walton absorbed a $2 billion loss of his Wal-Mart shares when the "Black Monday" stockmarket crash occurred. However, with more than $4 billion left, Walton was still at the top of the list when *Forbes* magazine ranked the richest people in America.

Pressure Point 8: Product Innovations

Product or service innovation requires a long-term view of business. While most companies opt for cash flow, innovators invest in future opportunities where returns are uncertain. To break new ground, you must look hard for opportunities. "If it ain't broke, don't fix it," is how most people conduct business. Yet innovators declare, "Even though it ain't broke, we can always make it better." To capitalize on your innovation, convert it into a marketable product with rapid diffusion into the marketplace. This is how Integrated Resources entered into hypergrowth.

Integrated Resources sold innovative investment products through several thousand independent financial planners. Once a tax shelter service for the wealthy, Integrated Resources repositioned itself in financial services with unique investment and insurance products.

Early on, Integrated Resources was known for its deep tax shelters. Wealthy customers accrued immediate lump sum tax-loss write-offs on cash that Integrated fronted them. For tax purposes, Integrated reported on a cash basis to show a negative cash flow. However, for financial reporting purposes, it projected profits and spread them evenly over the life of the property.

Integrated Resources specialized in privately placed net lease commercial real estate limited partnerships. Its innovations were closely tied to loose tax laws for high-bracket taxpayers. When legislators eliminated the markets for commercial real estate investments and deep tax shelters, Integrated Resources accelerated its shift toward a new generation of investment products. It created variable and universal life insurance products that gave policyholders insurance protection and tax-free access to the funds.

Integrated Resources completed its shift into financial services with state-of-the-art investment products. These innovative offerings gave Integrated Resources the most diversified portfolio of investment and insurance programs in the industry.

Because Integrated Resources paid few taxes and received little benefit from interest payments, it relied heavily on preferred stock offerings to finance its negative operating cash flow. However, burgeoning sales of its insurance-related products transformed Integrated's profile of receivables.

Integrated Resources emerged as a financial services leader through its innovative investment product. It came to manage more than $16 billion of assets on behalf of some 350,000 investors. Under radical market conditions, Selig Zises molded Integrated Resources into the twenty-second largest financial services company in the world during its hypergrowth decade.

Pressure Point 9: Pareto's Law

The nineteenth-century Italian economist Wilfredo Pareto declared that the top 20 percent of your customers generate 80 percent of your revenue. The Pareto Maldistribution Curve, commonly referred to as the 80/20 rule, recommends that you invest your first marketing dollars where they will bring the best return—with the top 20 percent. To find Pareto's 80/20 relationship, rank order your customers from highest to lowest by billings. Multiply the total number of customers by 0.20 and locate that point in the rankings. Total the revenue generated by this top 20 percent. Then divide this figure by your company's total revenue. Chances are your revenue from the top 20 percent will add up to 80 percent of the total.

Leslie Wexner figured out that the top 20 percent of The Limited's products generated 80 percent of its sales. In line with Pareto's Law, Wexner offered only those fashions that comprised 80 percent of fashion revenues.

Wexner started The Limited with a $5,000 loan from an aunt. He decided to limit his selection of clothes to just sportswear. So he designed medium-priced apparel to compliment the tastes and styles of the contemporary woman.

The Limited's annual sales soon exceeded $1 billion. With Wexner's 80/20 formula in place, he then acquired other stores that complimented his formula. Wexner acquired, then merged Pic-A-Dilly into Sizes Unlimited. He also took over the 770-store Lerner chain. Just three years after he broke the billion-dollar barrier, Wexner's sales surpassed $3 billion and The Limited ranked first among specialty retailers for sales growth, return on equity, and earnings per share. After Wexner's chain topped 3,000 stores, he entered the men's market and the children's market, again, by offering just the 20 percent of the items that generated 80 percent of the sales.

In a curious but revealing move, Wexner acquired the one and only Henri Bendel store located in New York City. Bendel's gave Wexner a chance to expand the exclusive fashion name into 40 markets. With Bendel's projected annual revenues approaching $700 million, Wexner's single year Bendel's sales would exceed its single store sales for an entire decade.

Leslie Wexner was profitable while selling his limited selection of merchandise because of his operating pace. Wexner's obsession with speed made him the fastest of all competitive retailers. His limited selection of private label merchandise is manufactured overseas and delivered to stores in two days through an integrated distribution system.

Leslie Wexner became America's dominant fashion apparel specialist with multiple retail formats because he rarely deviated from Pareto's Law. Focusing on the 20 percent of the merchandise that generated 80 percent of his sales made Wexner a specialty retail pioneer.

Pressure Point 10: Time Floats

A time float represents the gap between a customer request and the time it takes a company to deliver its solution. With new technology, improved distribution, and competitive services, time floats have been dramatically reduced and, in some cases, totally eliminated. Collapsing the time float will help you exploit new opportunities, reduce inventories, cut manufacturing costs, improve productivity, enhance communications, and provide access to restricted markets.

Fred Smith was sure that the passenger route system used by air freight shippers was wrong for freight distribution. He recognized that collapsing the time float when delivering products and information would be the next wave of America's Industrial Revolution. Smith figured that if people had overnight delivery they would like it and come to depend on it. So he invested his $4 million inheritance to launch Federal Express.

Federal Express was designed to help manufacturers eliminate the delays and expense of maintaining multiple warehouse inventories. Fred Smith targeted 37,000 companies in the 100 leading U.S. markets that accounted for 84 percent of all domestic air shipments. He figured that capturing 1 percent of this air freight market could support his company. Yet, Federal Express needed an infrastructure of planes, vans, and personnel in place from the outset in order to succeed.

It seemed like Federal Express would never get off the ground. It experienced operating losses from its inception through month 40. Employees loyal to their struggling leader were known to hock their watches just to buy a tank of gas. Then one afternoon, in an impulsive act, Smith flew to Las Vegas with a few hundred dollars and gambled for his payroll. When he won $27,000, it was a sign of good things to come.

So Fred Smith went on an 18-month-long fund-raising campaign that generated $52 million in new capital from blue-ribbon investors and aggressive banks. His next two years were spent lobbying Congress to drop air cargo restrictions imposed by the Civil Aeronautics Act of 1938.

With fresh capital and deregulated airways, Fred Smith upgraded his fleet of aircraft to 727s. His expanded carrying capacity improved Federal's service to its rapidly growing customer base.

Federal Express collapsed the time float with next-day express delivery. Fred Smith's absolutely, positively, overnight concept finally caught on and the company became the logistics arm for a burgeoning service economy. When its hypergrowth decade ended, Federal Express sales surpassed $5 billion in revenues.

Pressure Point 11: Design Defects

Isolating design defects creates another hypergrowth pressure point. When you find a weakness in the strength of a competitor, you can unravel its entire product line. In the computer industry, systems software, for example, was designed to improve a computer's operating efficiency. It soon evolved from simple instructions into highly influential designs that defined the boundaries of a computer's performance.

Computer Associates, in fact, was founded on the premise that within IBM's software systems there were many design defects. So Charles Wang addressed the defects with systems software that improved the performance of IBM mainframe computers. The company's first and most successful product, CA-SORT, was 25 percent faster and used 50 percent fewer resources than the IBM sort product it replaced. Following a series of acquisitions and internally developed products, Computer Associates carried software products for all the major IBM operating system environments including MVS, VM, and VSE.

Businesses began to realize the benefits of buying packaged solutions rather than developing them internally. Computer Associates fueled expansion of the applications software market by adding new packages to its inventory. Computer Associates was particularly well-shielded from its biggest competitor. IBM couldn't easily sell products that pointed out weaknesses in its own designs.

As data processing costs escalated, top management demanded that the corporate data center get more output for less money. At the same time, the migration to distributed data processing further complicated hardware and software purchasing decisions. Computer Associates positioned itself as a recession-proof business since data managers buy product enhancements in tough times rather than purchase new computers. Even as mainframe sales growth slowed, Computer Associates had plenty of room to cross-sell and upgrade its clients, which licensed an average of four products each.

Mainframe computer software accounts for 80 percent of Wang's business. In less than a decade Computer Associates became the leading independent software company in the world. With a portfolio of more than 200 different products installed in over 100,000 client sites, Computer Associates services 90 percent of the Fortune 500.

Computer Associates exploited the design defect pressure point to become the first software company to top $1 billion in annual sales. Computer Associates' secret to exploiting design defects was incorporating a singular view of software rather than one defined by hardware configurations or product functionality.

Pressure Point 12: Industry Monopolies

A monopoly forms when only one seller exists and no substitutes for a product are available. Monopolies typically form in industries where entry barriers are high. The controlling company resists innovation and charges higher prices than found in a competitive market. American Telephone and Telegraph, for example, had a near-perfect monopoly on long distance telephone service for a century. Antitrust laws were written to keep an industry like telecommunications from becoming so concentrated that a single company would dominate the market.

Bill McGowan stumbled upon a company that had the potential to break-up the powerful long distance monopoly. Jack Goeken owned and operated nine microwave stations between Chicago and St. Louis. McGowan saw an opportunity to expand this network into a nationwide long distance phone company. When visionary Goeken gave in to financeer McGowan, it mirrored the relationship a century earlier when Alexander Graham Bell turned control of his telephone over to Theodore Vail, who went on to create the AT&T monopoly.

Taking charge of MCI, McGowan visited the reading room of the Federal Communications Commission in Washington, DC, where he found plenty of documentation that legitimized monopolies for local telephone service. What he did not find was a piece of paper that granted AT&T a legal monopoly on long distance telephone service. Armed with that knowledge, Bill McGowan entered into a 17-year legal battle to break up the largest monopoly in American business history.

The FCC ruled in McGowan's favor saying that any business that was financially, technically, and legally qualified could enter the interstate telecommunications transmission market. AT&T was ordered by the FCC to provide all necessary local interconnections and anxiously watched MCI chip away at its customer base. AT&T then closed local connections so MCI's long distance calls could not be completed. This violated antitrust laws.

McGowan focused on the antitrust activities of AT&T because the court system was the only viable way to dismantle the monopoly. Congress would not get involved since AT&T had more than a million employees and a strong lobbying arm. The FCC didn't have the power to declare the monopoly illegal. So that left the judicial system and the burden on McGowan to prove that AT&T was violating antitrust laws.

AT&T's illegal efforts to keep MCI from competing led the FCC to strip AT&T of its exclusivity on long distance calls and telephone equipment. The Justice Department then dealt the crushing blow with its antitrust decision that forced the break-up of the monopoly and awarded MCI $1.8 billion in damages. AT&T appealed and the damages were later reduced to $113 million.

Once the monopoly was dismantled, MCI had to compete to survive. So McGowan directed MCI's sales effort at the 1 percent of American companies that had accounted for more than 40 percent of the long distance revenues. Within three years of the divestiture, long distance rates decreased 30 percent and MCI posted $4 billion in sales. MCI's efforts to eliminate the telephone monopoly spawned more than 300 new long distance competitors.

Pressure Point 13: Technology Integration

Once microcomputers became a standard office fixture, companies focused on how to tie them together. Technology integration let computer users share resources, communicate via electronic mail, and access reports from their mainframes. The technology integration pressure point involves comprehensive support through implementation, consultation, documentation, training, diagnostics, and follow-up services.

Birth of the personal computer spawned thousands of computer specialty stores. They filled the gap between consumer electronics shops and the manufacturer salesforce. Businessland steered clear of the retail market and focused instead on servicing America's 1,000 largest companies.

Businessland specialized in the design of local area networks (LANs) that connect personal computers to mainframes. As a result, they sold more PCs, networks, and software to more corporations, faster than any other computer store. Total revenues from Businessland's 108 units surpassed $1 billion by its eighth year in business.

To improve integration effectiveness, David Norman invested millions of dollars each year to train his engineers, salesforce, and support staff. While its competitors handled mostly IBM, Compaq, and Apple computers, Businessland integrated newer models including NeXT, Wyse, and Zenith Technologies.

Selling to Fortune 1,000 corporations forced Businessland to survive on thin margins. David Norman combined economies of scale with efficient order handling to produce profits. Low prices on computers got people into Businessland stores. Once inside, Norman sold them higher margin items such as software, modems, and supplies.

During its hypergrowth era, Businessland got caught between being a rock-bottom discounter and a value-added integrator. Norman promoted Businessland's network integration and many customers paid higher prices for the service. Yet, the majority of the market simply wanted its low prices and prompt delivery. As a result, less than 10 percent of Businessland's revenues came from value-added services.

As its hypergrowth decade came to a close, slowing sales of powerful high-end computers forced Businessland to cap discounts, lower commissions, layoff staff, fire its sales and marketing VPs, and change from expensive store-fronts to branch offices. Nonetheless, David Norman stayed focused on technology integration to differentiate Businessland from the competition.

Pressure Point 14: Pent-Up Demand

In the United States, more than 500,000 manufacturers, 600,000 wholesalers, and 2.5 million retailers serve the needs of 250 million consumers. Pent-up demand, from a consumer standpoint, starts with awareness of product attributes. Next, consumers develop a preference for one brand over another. Finally, the first company to create a new product category becomes the dominant player—if it can master the manufacturing, marketing, and distribution functions.

The personal computer industry's annual growth rate hovered around 90 percent for nearly a decade. Apple Computer responded to the market's pent-up demand with an extensive line of personal computers, communications products, peripherals, and systems software.

By age 25, Steve Jobs had attained a net worth surpassing $400 million as his company fed the pent-up demand for personal computers. He attacked the business market with the Macintosh and Apple II families. The Macintosh product line was embraced by businesses because of its desktop publishing, 3-D design simulation, word processing, and information management capabilities.

Apple's early success in education resulted from building computers that empowered individuals. It captured 60 percent of the kindergarten through 12-grade market and one-third of the college market, as schools purchased about 500,000 personal computers annually.

To meet the pent-up demand for interoperability in multi-vendor environments, Apple created its Information Systems and Technology Group, Customer Satisfaction Group, and Apple Integrated Systems Group. These groups provided customers with sophisticated networking and communication capabilities.

In the beginning, Apple sold PCs through independent manufacturer representatives. Apple didn't have the resources to bankroll a direct-to-dealer salesforce. However, once it achieved critical mass, Apple ran ads in major newspapers and trade publications to recruit 350 of the best salespeople in the country. More than 12,000 applications flowed in to Apple headquarters. So Apple designed a three-week crash course called Sell With Apple Training (SWAT). The hand-picked sales team was merged into the distribution organization. Together, they were responsible for getting Apple products from the factory to the customer.

Apple created its University Consortium program that sold computers directly to students, bypassing the dealer network. It placed discounted Macintosh computers into the hands of thousands of students who were preparing to enter the business world. Many of these students became part of Apple's user groups that solved practical problems associated with personal computing. Apple tracked computer owners, tested new products, and promoted advanced software development through its user groups.

Positioned as the computer for "the rest of us" the Macintosh brought computing power to people who never considered personal computers before. Steve Jobs fed the pent-up market demand as people learned to use a Macintosh in less than an hour.

Pressure Point 15: Manufacturing Intermediaries

Manufacturers often farm out aspects of product development to intermediaries as a way to keep their costs down and accelerate production. In those industries where short lifecycles prevail, manufacturing intermediaries like Seagate Technology stimulate innovation and spark volatility.

After 22 years of designing disk drives for other companies, Alan Shugart decided to work for himself. He started Seagate Technology and built data storage devices to save, then retrieve, millions of bits of computerized data. To achieve hypergrowth as a manufacturing intermediary, Seagate focused on becoming the low-cost producer of hard disk drives.

Seagate was the first intermediary to introduce the 5 1/4-inch disk drive. It produced huge volumes, then passed on incremental savings through lower prices. Seagate always looked for new ways to reduce component costs. Management teams frequently analyzed each part of a disk drive and ordered vendors to stop shipments unless they provided price concessions.

Efficient manufacturing was only half of Seagate's success formula. They also expanded distribution channels to include computer dealers and value-added resellers. A major breakthrough for Seagate occurred when a small company bought stripped down IBM PCs, installed Seagate's drives, then resold the more powerful version at bargain rates. Seagate showed other wholesalers how to open up IBM computers and install its hard disk drives. As a result, Seagate's revenues doubled the next year and its stock price tripled.

Original equipment manufacturers (OEM) account for a large portion of Seagate sales. Cracking the OEM network took hard work and creative selling. While holding a virtual lock on IBM, Seagate made inroads with Apple Computer through aggressive price cutting, which eroded its competitor's market share. As a low-cost producer, Seagate learned how to make money in an industry where the growth rate dropped by two-thirds in just two years.

Manufacturing intermediaries must adjust quickly to new products. While Seagate was celebrating a record year of production, its customers began buying a new 20-megabyte disk drive from competitors. When IBM's product supplier shipped faulty disk drives, Seagate seized the opportunity to create a superfast prototype using a new technology. Seagate received the large volume order based on the prototype's success and its competitor went out of business.

EXPLOIT ANOMALIES AT PRESSURE POINTS

To generate hypergrowth, learn to recognize anomalies at pressure points. Then find a way to align your products and services with these emerging opportunities. This will generate new levels of innovation, productivity, and profitability.

Spotting anomalies at pressure points is just the beginning. You need to get your product into the hands of the core group, luminaries, analysts, dealers, and the press so the word gets out. These market makers discern new ideas and spurn mediocrity. When they embrace your product, the rest of the market will follow.

Remember, the core group is tightly knit, makes informed choices, and recommends what it uses. The core group also lives for technical specifications, features, and benefits. They love in-depth product information. Therefore, when targeting your core group, load up your brochures, user manuals, and point-of-purchase materials with an abundance of technical data.

4

Know What You Do Best, Then Do It Better Than Anyone Else

While identifying anomalies and pressure points is an integral part of hypergrowth, it is only the start. Your next step is to develop a game plan that sets you up for success. This requires knowing what you do best.

The founders of hypergrowth companies all knew what they did best . . . then they did it better than anyone else. Their exposure to customers, competitors, bankers, manufacturers, vendors, lawyers, retailers, distributors, the media, and others revealed their personal strengths that helped them form enduring business values.

Exposure is different from experience; none of these executives had ever experienced hypergrowth before. Yet, they had all been exposed to the business dynamics that ultimately led their ventures into hypergrowth. Exposure creates opportunity.

Upon settling into what they did best, the tangible evidences of "doing it better than anyone else" were increased revenues and dominant market share. However, the early signs of hypergrowth success began with business qualities described in terms of "design advantages," "zero defects,"

51

"intensive training," "innovative approaches," "efficiency break-throughs," "broad appeal," and "conceptual retooling."

Once you know what you do best, your desire to be the best will express itself in the continual search for the highest performance level in the marketplace. Know what you do best, then do it better than anyone else and you may find yourself joining the Hypergrowth Hall of Fame.

KNOW WHAT YOU DO BEST

Hypergrowth requires more skills than any one executive brings to the table. So the successful executives isolate what they do best and stick with it. All other tasks and responsibilities get delegated to partners, associates, or staff. To know what you do best, take an inventory of your exposures, interests, mentors, hobbies, and associations.

Step 1: Describe Your Significant Business Exposures

Organize a section of a notebook and call it "exposures." Then list business insights gleaned from involvement in significant activities such as incorporating a business, obtaining a line of credit, getting news coverage, importing a product, and so on.

Step 2: List Your Business Strengths

In another section of the notebook called "strengths," list the business activities you have excelled in. If you find that you naturally migrate toward these tasks under stress, there is a good chance the activities express hidden aptitudes. Consider these your "places of strength" and, like muscles, exercise them.

Step 3: List Your Mentor Lessons

In a third section of your notebook entitled "mentors," describe the business lessons imparted to you as an understudy to a mentor. Describe with clarity the circumstances under which the principles were learned.

Step 4: Define Your Hobbies

Create a notebook section called "hobbies." List the activities you engage in for pleasure. Consider the time devoted to your hobbies. Then ask yourself how you can rechannel this time into a business mission that provides solutions to unsolved problems.

Step 5: Detail Your Network

Finally, in a section entitled "network," list every friend, associate, and professional you know (or know about) whose skills could someday be harnessed for your hypergrowth venture.

Make this a dynamic notebook. Update it constantly. As you gain new ideas and insights, juxtapose them to piece your hypergrowth puzzle together.

DO WHAT YOU DO BEST BETTER THAN ANYONE ELSE

Once you know what you do best, you have to figure out how to do it better than anyone else. This is no easy task. However, the four key principles imparted by successful hypergrowth executives include:

- *Become a visionary.*
  Hypergrowth is not just another goal-setting exercise. It requires an all-consuming vision for a cause. Successful visionaries make uncompromising commitments to meet universal needs. For example, Bernard Marcus committed himself to help Home Depot's do-it-yourself customers fight inflation; Fred Smith created Federal Express as social changes brought about the need for a new distribution

infrastructure; John Malone molded TCI to deliver the best value in entertainment. These hypergrowth visionaries then gathered top talent and financial resources to help fulfill their missions.

- *Take aim at the leader.*
"Doing it better than anyone else" assumes you've become the market leader. If you are not yet on top, set your sights on toppling the market leader. Yet, never compete head-to-head. Your first and safest strategy is to find a market niche that is underserved or ignored by the market leader. Pick a fringe area that has growth potential, then service its unmet needs.

When Paul Fireman introduced his aerobics shoe to the U.S. athletic shoe market, Nike was the running shoe leader with $636 million in sales. Fireman was no "ego-tripping fool" while recording sales of just $13 million. He played it smart and exploited the fringe niches. His aerobics, basketball, volleyball, and walking shoe designs got Reebok on the fast track. Just five years later, Reebok registered sales of $1.4 billion and left Nike in the dust with sales of $877 million.

The second, more risky strategy requires you to shoot for the Achilles' heel of the market leader. Achilles, the hero of Homer's *Illiad,* was considered invulnerable. However, he was eventually struck down when an arrow penetrated his heel.

Rod Canion took the Achilles' heel approach with IBM, whose market value was greater than the entire capitalization of all the companies traded on the American Stock Exchange. He didn't go head-to-head with a mainframe product. Instead, Canion found a manufacturing and design "heel" in the world's biggest computer company. He attacked its newest product, the personal computer, by introducing the first portable computer that was compatible with IBM's PC.

IBM could not ignore Compaq's growing reputation and superior products. So IBM spent a year retooling, then introduced its own portable computer. IBM's launch delay and poor product design gave the marketplace two good reasons to continue to buy from Compaq.

The risk/reward factor is significant when you attack the weakness of a market leader. By going for the Achilles' heel, you'll either strike down the leader if you're right, or get crushed under its foot if you're wrong.

- *Excel in "3-D."*
Hypergrowth companies display 3-D superiority when it comes to design, distribution, and differentiation: Leslie Wexner, for example, *designs* his own brand-name clothes copied from the latest fashion trends. The Limited's integrated *distribution* system serves as the industry model for speed and efficiency. Wexner then *differentiates* his trendy "knock-off" fashions by selling them through 3,095 stores in nine different store formats.

    With design, never introduce products or services unless they display technical or functional superiority. With distribution, provide the fastest, most reliable service and you can price products at a premium. Finally, differentiate your product or service so you can highlight its superior benefits when compared with the competition. Remember, products in hypergrowth markets are never presented as commodities.

- *After you're the best, pour it on!*
Getting to the top is hard, staying there is profitable. Don't sell out; instead pour it on. Accept nothing less from your venture than total market dominance. Keep growing and adding new products. Accelerate distribution and find better manufacturing sources. Lower your prices and add new customers. Enjoy your hypergrowth success . . . it's your reward for combining creative genius with hard work.

CRITICAL SUCCESS FACTORS OF HYPERGROWTH

Critical success factors (CSFs) are to a business, what vital organs are to a human body. Healthy individuals have fully functioning vital organs that include the heart, kidneys, liver, and brain. In a similar manner, the strengths of hypergrowth companies are concentrated within their fully functioning critical success factors, without which their businesses could not survive.

Hypergrowth results when companies work from their strengths to meet changing needs in the marketplace. Focusing on these CSFs improves an organization's design and operational effectiveness. However, hypergrowth is not an automatic biproduct of identifying your critical success factors. Your relative strengths must still interface with anomalies at pressure points within fast-changing markets. This is why, under the same market conditions, one company experiences hypergrowth while its competitors don't.

Managing a company's critical success factors is the single most important responsibility of a corporate officer. Focusing on CSFs helps a company invest its resources to identify and exploit emerging hypergrowth opportunities. Locating a company's critical success factors, however, is not always easy. The first step is to visualize the business as a whole, from raw materials all the way through to customer service.

THE OPERATIONS OVERVIEW

In order to develop this big picture, an operations overview needs to be created. Your operations flow chart will include a business starting point, the critical success factors, key activities that interface with the CSFs, directional flow of activities, and a point of contact with customers.

The operations overview can depict a company from a variety of angles. This is advantageous since often only minor adjustments in strategy can facilitate a rush of new growth activity. Such a design also helps a business synergistically utilize its relative strengths to achieve maximum penetration in the marketplace. Finally, achieving a consensus regarding your organization's operations overview focuses resources and energies on the hypergrowth opportunity.

Most companies, however, stumble into hypergrowth lacking

the resources to take full advantage of the opportunity. In these cases, a clear operations overview with well-defined critical success factors dictates the most effective allocation of time, financial, and personnel resources. Knowing where to invest scarce assets to bring about their best return is the secret to placing a company on the path to hypergrowth.

Designing your operations overview requires a creative visual imagination. You will need trial-and-error analysis to figure out exactly how your company functions in hypergrowth. Your operational design should eliminate barriers and bottlenecks so success flows. Remember, critical success factors of your operations overview must stay healthy and strong in order for your enterprise to survive and thrive in hypergrowth.

The goal of this exercise is to help you know what you do best, so you can do it better than anyone else. Study carefully the operations overviews and critical success factors of these hypergrowth companies and overlay the principles of their success to your venture.

A Computer Manufacturer   Rod Canion founded Compaq, but only after years of discontent. He dropped out of the University of Houston when he couldn't find a Ph.D. dissertation topic. He then went to work for Texas Instruments as a business unit manager. Rod Canion resigned after 13 years to challenge IBM's products with his portable computer design. As you study America's fastest growing start-up (Figure 4.1), keep in mind that Compaq has sold more than 30 million high performance, personal computers through more than 3,000 authorized dealers in 40 countries.

Compaq is a public company located in Houston, Texas, which trades on the New York, Midwest, and Pacific Stock Exchanges (symbol: CPQ) with 5,458 shareholders of record. It is staffed by 4,000 full-time employees. After just eight years in business, Compaq's sales grew from 0 to $2.9 billion.

- *Critical Success Factor 1: Research & Development.*
  Compaq conducted extensive research to identify problems of personal computer users. In five years, Compaq's research and development budget burgeoned from $3.7

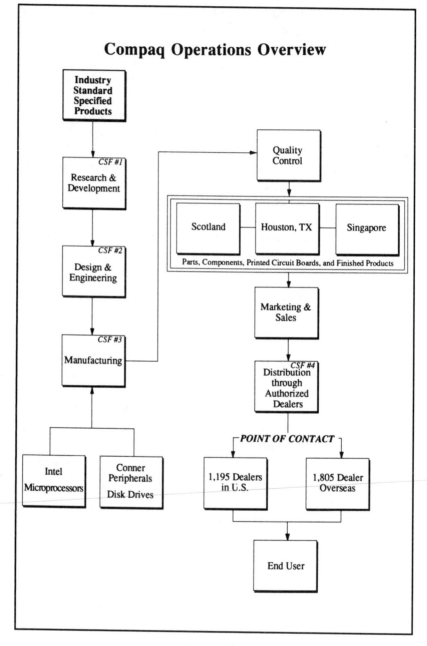

Figure 4.1

million to $47 million. This investment, in most cases, simply determined a clear market need among experienced computer users who wanted top performance and IBM compatibility.

- *Critical Success Factor 2: Design & Engineering.*
  Compaq engineers introduced a new personal computer design every nine months, with expanded functional capabilities. For example, its Deskpro 386 was hailed as "the most advanced personal computer in the industry" upon its introduction since it accomplished many tasks of a mini-computer but at lower costs.

- *Critical Success Factor 3: Manufacturing.*
  Compaq adhered to a basic formula: Build the right product, then get it to market quickly. Compaq's manufacturing systems are closely monitored to meet the strictest quality standards in the industry since Rod Canion demands zero defects from his products.

- *Critical Success Factor 4: Distribution.*
  Lacking resources for a salesforce and unenthusiastic about "third party" resellers, Rod Canion aggressively pursued the dealer network. He hired away the former sales manager of the IBM PC team who helped differentiate Compaq from the other 100 computer companies aimed at the business market.

A Computer Retailer   David Norman had been a fighter pilot in the Navy, then earned a masters degree from Stanford University. His aptitudes and interests led him to start a computer retail company following a successful research career. In his value-added environment, Norman and his staff integrate microcomputer products from selected manufacturers to create custom-designed computer systems. As you analyze America's leading computer retailer (Figure 4.2), remember that Businessland sold so many computers and value-added services that it became the fastest growing and largest publicly held computer chain in America.

Businessland is a public company located in San Jose,

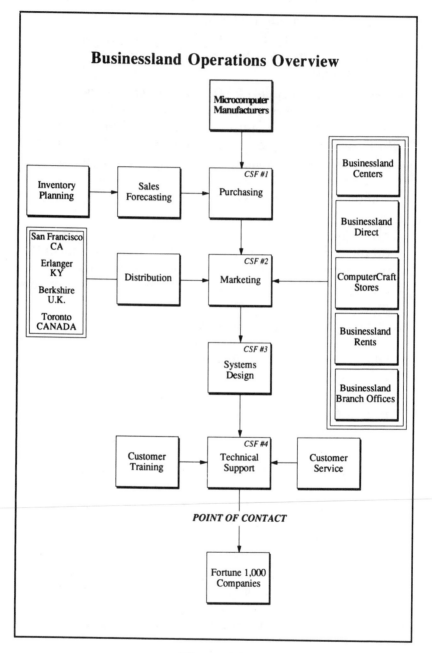

Businessland Operations Overview

Microcomputer Manufacturers

Inventory Planning → Sales Forecasting → *CSF #1* Purchasing

Businessland Centers

Businessland Direct

ComputerCraft Stores

Businessland Rents

Businessland Branch Offices

San Francisco CA / Erlanger KY / Berkshire U.K. / Toronto CANADA → Distribution → *CSF #2* Marketing

CSF #3 Systems Design

Customer Training → *CSF #4* Technical Support ← Customer Service

POINT OF CONTACT

Fortune 1,000 Companies

Figure 4.2

California, which trades on the New York Stock Exchange (symbol: BLI) with 1,604 shareholders of record. It is staffed by 3,452 employees worldwide. Just eight years after starting up, Businessland achieved sales of $1.2 billion.

- *Critical Success Factor 1: Purchasing.*
  Businessland provides a wide selection of business automation equipment that includes advanced microcomputer systems, networking peripherals, workstations, printers, modems, software, and supplies. It purchases products from IBM, Apple, Compaq, Hewlett-Packard, OKI Data Group, Microsoft, Lotus, Ashton-Tate, Multimate, and many other microcomputer-related companies.

- *Critical Success Factor 2: Marketing.*
  Businessland's catalogs offer more than 9,000 different products through a toll-free ordering system. Its government sales group established one-stop shopping for computers and services which simplified the procurement process. Businessland's strategic partnerships also help customers evaluate future technologies and how to implement them into the corporate setting.

- *Critical Success Factor 3: Systems Design.*
  Highly skilled personnel design local area networks to connect different computers into company-wide information systems. Businessland provides system configurations, system burn-in, and other value-added design functions.

- *Critical Success Factor 4: Support.*
  Businessland's technical support team consists of more than 1,000 trained personnel who deliver, install, and train customers in the use of PC equipment. Businessland's staff handles more than 25,000 phone calls each year over its Solution Line. David Norman's full-time instructors teach classes on all of Businessland's products and services in conjunction with its Television and Technology Forums, which analyze industry trends and answer customer questions.

A Shoe Manufacturer and Wholesaler   Paul Fireman was the vice-president for a family-owned camping equipment distributor when his manufacturers began dealing directly with retailers. So he went searching for new products and new niches. While at a Chicago trade show, Fireman obtained the North American rights to manufacture and market Reeboks. As you consider its operations overview (Figure 4.3), keep in mind that Reebok designs, manufactures, and markets 250 different models of shoes in 12 footwear categories to account for one-third of the 100 million pairs of athletic shoes sold annually in America.

Reebok is a public company located in Canton, Massachusetts, that trades on the New York Stock Exchange (symbol: RBK) with 21,000 shareholders of record. It is staffed with 2,400 non-union employees. In its decade of hypergrowth, Reebok sales increased from $1 million to $1.8 billion.

- *Critical Success Factor 1: Research & Development.*
  Reebok research focuses on fashion as well as function. When consumers reported excess stress on ankle and metatarsal bones, Reebok responded with an innovative sole design. When consumers complained about blisters, Reebok designed its shoes with reinforced garment leather to eliminate the break-in period.

- *Critical Success Factor 2: Manufacturing.*
  To cope with risks of foreign manufacturing, Reebok rewrote its contracts to include rejections and financial penalties when suppliers did not meet quality specifications. Then Fireman added geographically diverse manufacturers that expanded Reebok's production capacity and improved its quality control.

- *Critical Success Factor 3: Marketing.*
  Reebok not only anticipated the aerobics market boom, they nurtured it through unsolicited endorsements by Bill Cosby, Bruce Springsteen, and Cybill Shepherd, who attended the Emmy Awards wearing orange Reeboks. Steve Jones influenced brand referencing when he set a world

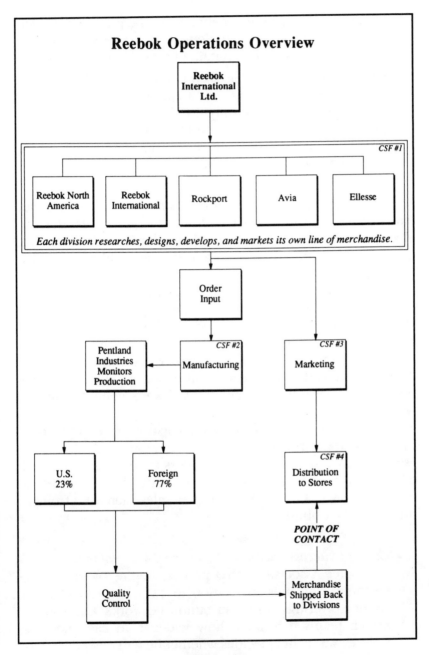

Figure 4.3

marathon record in his Reeboks. On the grass roots level, Reebok distributed newsletters, sponsored research, hosted seminars, and maintained a certification program.

- *Critical Success Factor 4: Distribution.*
  Since consumers judge shoe brand quality by distribution quality, Reebok picked only the best merchandisers for its products. Reebok's 5,000 nationwide distributors included pro shops, athletic specialty stores, sporting goods stores, and upscale department stores.

A Computer Software Designer   Software design was not part of Charles Wang's early childhood experiences. Born in Shanghai, China, Wang immigrated to the United States with his parents and two brothers when he was a child. As a computer programmer just out of college, Wang stumbled upon a Swiss software company called Computer Associates, whose products made IBM mainframe systems work more efficiently. Wang obtained half of the U.S. rights to the company and eventually purchased the entire company. As you study its operations overview (Figure 4.4), remember that through internal development and corporate acquisitions, Computer Associates became the largest independent software company in the world.

Computer Associates is a public company located in Garden City, New York, that trades on the New York Stock Exchange (symbol: CA) with 11,000 shareholders of record. It has 6,500 employees, more than half in sales and marketing. In its decade of hypergrowth, Computer Associates sales increased from $7 million to $1.1 billion.

- *Critical Success Factor 1: Research & Development.*
  Computer Associates' R&D process begins by examining customer demands in relation to existing product lines, service offerings, and distribution networks. Once its research teams determine how widespread each need is, Charles Wang then decides whether he will meet the needs with acquired technology or develop it in-house.

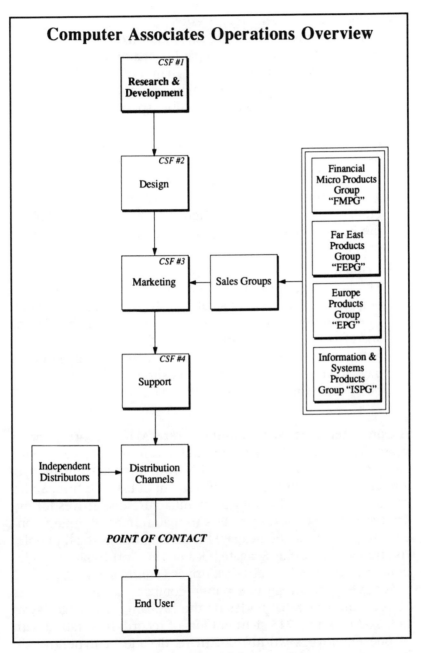

Figure 4.4

- *Critical Success Factor 2: Design.*
  Computer Associates designs standardized software products for IBM and IBM-compatible mainframe, mini, and microcomputer systems. More than 1,500 employees engage in the design of its products to provide total software solutions across the widest possible spectrum of use.
- *Critical Success Factor 3: Marketing.*
  Computer Associates markets its products on a worldwide basis primarily through its 3,300 sales and presales support personnel. The marketing effort is organized into four groups: the Information and Systems Products Group (ISPF), the Financial and Micro Products Group (FMPG), the Europe Products Group (EPG), and the Far East Products Group (FEPG).
- *Critical Success Factor 4: Support.*
  The licensing of Computer Associates software is only the beginning of the client's relationship with the company. Client support guarantees the installation, implementation, and effective use of its products with a worldwide support network through 100 offices, in 22 countries, 24-hours-a-day, 365-days-a-year. CA takes its support obligations seriously since future sales are built on customer loyalty.

A Computer Accessory Manufacturer Alan Shugart spent 18 years designing disk drives for IBM and four more years with Memorex before striking out on his own. After starting Shugart Associates, Alan Shugart was pushed out of his own firm. So he created Seagate Technology to manufacture disk drives for every type of computer, from PCs to mainframes. Running contrary to popular belief, Seagate became all things to all people. Its strategy paid off as Seagate became the world's largest independent maker of PC hard-disk drives (Figure 4.5).

Seagate Technology is a public company located in Scotts Valley, California, that trades on the NASDAQ Exchange (symbol: SGAT) with 7,713 shareholders of record. It is staffed with 39,000 employees worldwide. In its decade of hypergrowth, Seagate sales increased from $10 million to $2.4 billion.

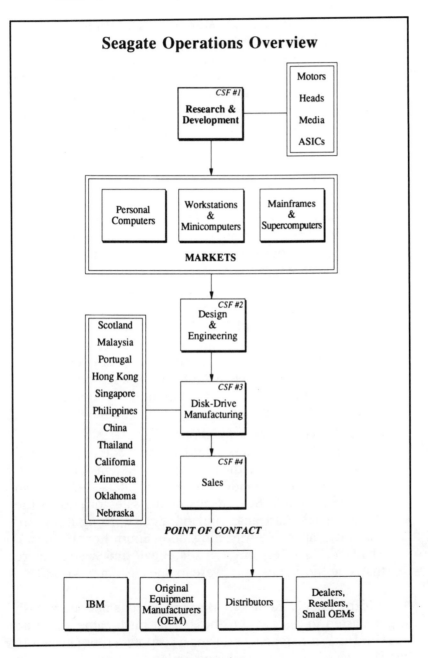

Figure 4.5

- *Critical Success Factor 1: Research & Development.*
  In the final three years of its hypergrowth decade, Seagate invested more than $205 million in research & development. Its investment focused on improving the bearing systems of motors; developing production processes for magneto-resistive heads; researching media to find higher performance materials; and developing application-specific integrated circuits (ASICs).

- *Critical Success Factor 2: Design & Engineering.*
  Seagate's design and engineering teams improved manufacturing processes to lower costs and increase volume production. In an industry characterized by rapid technological change and short lifecycles, Seagate designers create new components, introduce new products, and integrate emerging technologies.

- *Critical Success Factor 3: Manufacturing.*
  Seagate established its manufacturing capacity in anticipation of market demand. The key elements of its manufacturing success include high-volume/low-cost assembly, vertical integration of critical components, key vendor relationships, and advanced manufacturing methods. Seagate maintains strict control over component technology, quality, availability, and costs.

- *Critical Success Factor 4: Sales.*
  Seagate sells its products to both original equipment manufacturers (OEMs) for their computer systems and to distributors, which include resellers, dealers, and system integrators. While Seagate maintains sales offices in the United States, Australia, England, France, Hong Kong, India, Italy, Japan, Norway, Singapore, South Korea, Taiwan, Thailand, West Germany, Canada, Brazil, and Sweden, more than one-third of its sales were to one customer—IBM.

A Building Supply Retailer   Bernard Marcus needed a push to get started in his own business. That push came when he was fired as a store manager during a corporate reorganization. Just five days later, he developed a plan for a retail store that combined low prices, high volume, and quality service. So he raised $2 million in venture capital, then searched the country for store sites close to do-it-yourselfers. Keep in mind as you analyze this operations overview (Figure 4.6), that each and every one of Home Depot's 118 retail do-it-yourself (DIY) warehouses required at least an $8 million investment to launch.

Home Depot is a public company located in Atlanta, Georgia, that trades on the New York Stock Exchange (symbol: HD) with 4,055 shareholders of record. It is staffed with 9,700 employees, 90 percent on a full-time basis. In its decade of hypergrowth, Home Depot sales increased from $22 million to $2.8 billion.

- *Critical Success Factor 1: Buying.*
  Initial buying decisions are made at the corporate level, then unit managers place virtually all reorders. Computerized sales records link product selection to market demand as up to 20 percent of Home Depot's inventory is customized for regional needs.

- *Critical Success Factor 2: Merchandising.*
  Home Depot's "Low Day-In, Day-Out" merchandising is reinforced by hundreds of loss-leader items for sale at or below cost. Home Depot's staff of tradesmen then offer in-store clinics on topics ranging from wallpapering to wiring, together with project-long assistance by phone.

- *Critical Success Factor 3: PIMS.*
  The installation of its Perpetual Inventory Management System (PIMS) improved Home Depot's annual inventory turns by nearly 20 percent, which lowered its inventory investment by $40 million. The PIMS reports highlight sales margins and evaluates merchandise based on sales and profitability.

- *Critical Success Factor 4: Management.*
  Home Depot management stays intimately involved with operations through frequent store visits, new location inspections, trips to competitive operations, and executive training. Top level executives evaluate alternative

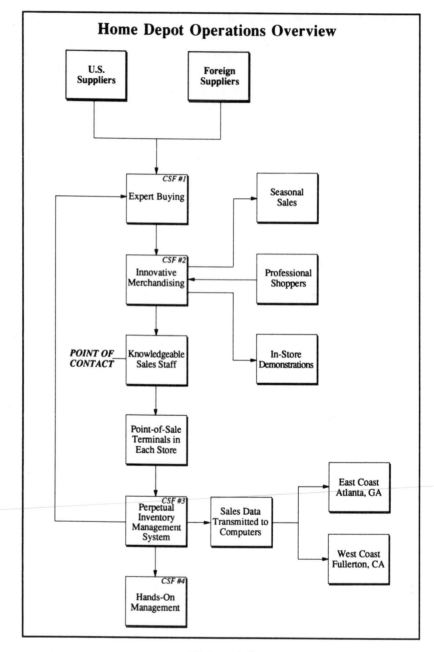

Figure 4.6

locations when real estate drives up the costs for primary new store sites.

A Clothing Designer and Wholesaler   Hypergrowth was not part of Liz Claiborne's agenda when she won a *Harper's Bazaar* design contest at age 21. Following apprenticeships with several New York designers, Liz was hired by Arthur Ortenberg, head of the junior-dress division at a women's sportwear company. Liz and Arthur fell in love, divorced their spouses, then married. While chief designer of the Youth Guild, Liz realized that the working woman needed more wardrobe options. So she started her own company. The Liz Claiborne operations overview (Figure 4.7) will help you understand how this dynamic company can introduce a new clothing line every eight weeks to meet the fashion demands of professional women.

Liz Claiborne, Inc. is a public company located in New York City, that trades on the New York Stock Exchange (symbol: LIZ) with 16,195 shareholders of record. It is staffed with 3,400 full-time employees worldwide. In its decade of hypergrowth, its sales increased from $79 million to $1.1 billion.

- *Critical Success Factor 1: Design.*
  Liz Claiborne's in-house design teams work closely with the sales, production, and merchandising staffs to prepare each collection. The designers also meet with major customers early in each design cycle to discuss retail trends and ways to maintain consumer loyalty.

- *Critical Success Factor 2: Production Administration.*
  Since Liz Claiborne does not own or operate production facilities, manufacturing is coordinated through 320 independent suppliers. The administrators interface with product engineering, pattern and sample making, production allocation, suppliers, and quality control to deliver its bimonthly fashion lines.

- *Critical Success Factor 3: Data Processing.*
  Liz Claiborne's computers record styles, colors, and sizes purchased weekly from a nationwide cross-section of

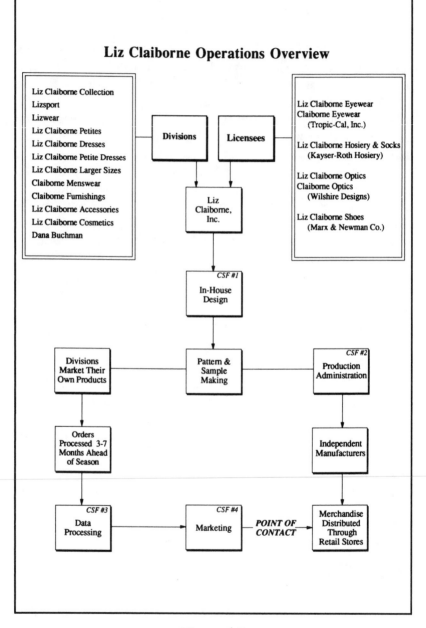

Figure 4.7

stores. Sales information is repackaged in dozens of ways to correlate consumer purchases with Claiborne merchandise through its proprietary Systematic Updated Retail Feedback (SURF) reports.

- *Critical Success Factor 4: Marketing.*
  Liz requires stores to give her a say in how they display her clothing, which achieved annual sales of $500 per square foot—three times the industry average. Liz Claiborne's cooperative advertising program matches a store's advertising expenditures up to 2 percent of its apparel purchases.

A Financial Services Company   Selig Zises worked with an equipment leasing company after graduating from college. Zises liked investing so he started Integrated Resources with his younger brother and a lifelong friend. Integrated Resources entered the overheated new-issues market when the three founders collectively raised $270,000. On its first day, Integrated's stock increased by 153 percent to establish a market value of $33 million. As you consider its operations overview (Figure 4.8), remember that Integrated Resources became a billion-dollar global company as a manufacturer and marketer of financial services and products.

Integrated Resources is a public company located in New York City, that trades on the New York Stock Exchange (symbol: IRE) with 1,700 shareholders of record. It is staffed with 3,750 employees and 4,100 independent sales agents. In its decade of hypergrowth, Integrated Resources' sales increased from $84 million to $1.7 billion.

- *Critical Success Factor 1: Insurance Carriers.*
  Integrated Resources transitioned from an investment company into one of the nation's largest insurance organizations through its strategic acquisitions over a five-year period. They purchased Provident Life Insurance for $14 million, Guardsman Life of Iowa for $29 million, and The Capitol Life Insurance Company for $64 million, allowing Integrated to sell insurance throughout the United States.

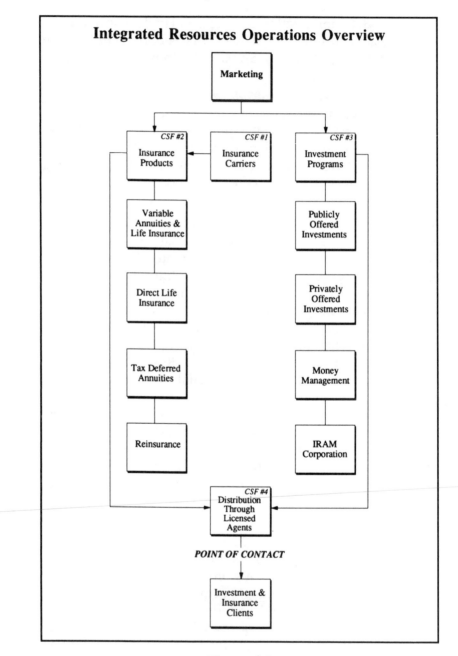

Figure 4.8

- *Critical Success Factor 2: Insurance Products.*
  At Integrated Resources, life insurance is considered a vital planning tool with tax deferral and capital growth potential. Its custom-designed products include interest-sensitive life insurance plans, variable annuities, variable life, tax sheltered annuities, pension and profit-sharing plans, key-person compensation, and charitable bequest programs.

- *Critical Success Factor 3: Investment Programs.*
  Integrated Resources Asset Management Corp. (IRAM) provides professional management of individual, corporate, and retirement plan portfolios. As America's leading portfolio management company, IRAM helped Integrated Resources become more fee-oriented and less volume-dependent.

- *Critical Success Factor 4: Distribution.*
  Integrated Resources established a nationwide distribution network comprised of 4,100 independent financial planners, hundreds of unaffiliated securities firms, and thousands of independent insurance agents. Integrated Resources Investment Centers provide financial products and services through banks and savings and loan associations while an international subsidiary distributes Integrated Resources products in Europe and the Far East.

A Computer Manufacturer   Steve Jobs founded Apple Computer at the age of 21 and recruited 26-year-old Steve Wozniak to assemble computer circuit boards. Their Apple I debuted at the Homebrew Computer Club on the campus of Stanford University. They then obtained a line of credit and produced their first batch of Apple computers. Hypergrowth resulted when Steve Jobs set out to change the world with his home-made computers. As you study America's hypergrowth pioneer (Figure 4.9), remember that while Apple preaches lofty ideals, it now functions as a Fortune 200 marketing machine with a goal to increase the wealth of its shareholders—more bottom-line ideals.

Apple Computer is a public company located in Cupertino, California, that trades on the NASDAQ Exchange (symbol: AAPL) with 34,266 shareholders of record. It is staffed by

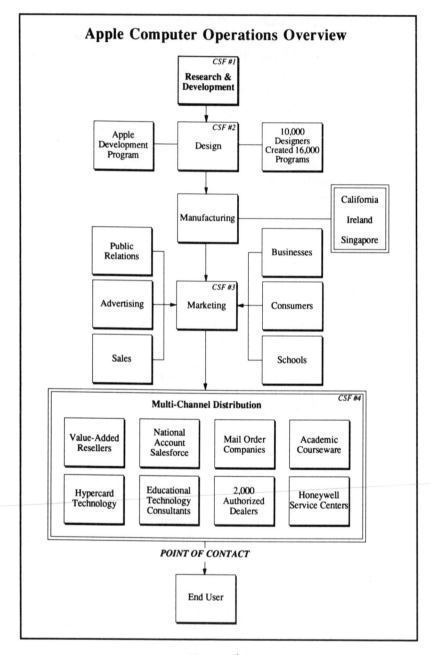

Figure 4.9

12,000 full-time and 2,500 part-time employees worldwide. The Apple Computer Company began from a garage with $1,350 in start-up capital and grew to more than $5.3 billion in sales by the end of its hypergrowth decade.

- *Critical Success Factor 1: Research & Development.*
  In the last three years of its hypergrowth decade, Apple Computer invested a total of $885 million on research and development. Apple's success hinged on its ability to adapt quickly to technological changes in the personal computer industry with innovative hardware, networking communications, and enhanced software products.
- *Critical Success Factor 2: Design.*
  Apple has more than 10,000 certified designers participating in the Apple Developer Program. They have designed more than 12,000 software programs for the Apple II and about 4,000 third-party software packages for the Macintosh computer.
- *Critical Success Factor 3: Marketing.*
  Apple, the first company to advertise personal computers in consumer magazines, became a household name by its fourth year in business as it registered an 80 percent public awareness rate. When they were excluded from the approved vendor lists at major corporations, Apple created a "Trojan Horse" that they called Desktop Publishing. This unique marketing ploy got the Macintosh computer into the advertising, communications, and marketing departments of most Fortune 500 companies.
- *Critical Success Factor 4: Distribution.*
  When it comes to distribution, Apple Computer can't seem to get enough. They open wide their distribution pipeline and blast products through it. The concept of controlled distribution has no place in Apple's delivery program. Apple offers many distribution options then lets its customers choose which channels to patronize. The secret to distribution success has been Apple's ability to create customer demand for its products.

A Cable Television Company   Bob Magness actually started Tele-Communications, Inc. (TCI) by building one of the early cable systems in Memphis, Texas. When John Malone, president of General Instruments' cable equipment division, extended credit to TCI, Bob Magness offered Malone part ownership in the struggling cable company. Keep in mind as you study this operations overview (Figure 4.10), that TCI became America's largest cable television company then split itself into separately managed subsidiaries to avoid an antitrust case.

Tele-Communications, Inc. is a public company located in Denver, Colorado, that trades on the NASDAQ Exchange (symbols: TCOMA & TCOMB) with 4,553 and 955 shareholders of record. It has 22,000 employees, with only 225 working from headquarters. In its decade of hypergrowth, TCI sales increased from $135 million to $3.0 billion.

- *Critical Success Factor 1: Programming.*
  TCI invested in more than 35 cable programming entities including The Discovery Channel, QVC Network, Black Entertainment Television, Turner Broadcasting System, and Think Entertainment. It also entered into joint ventures to produce regional sporting events.

- *Critical Success Factor 2: Operations.*
  John Malone decentralized TCI before federal regulators stepped in to limit the size of his cable company. He divided TCI into six operating divisions with independent marketing, accounting, and engineering departments to provide more responsive support in local markets.

- *Critical Success Factor 3: Communications.*
  When TCI acquired control of United Artists Communications, Inc., John Malone gained an additional 231 cable television systems serving 753,000 subscribers at half the going rate. He also took control of the nation's largest theater chain with 2,049 screens and appreciating real estate holdings.

- *Critical Success Factor 4: Distribution.*
  TCI distributes programming services to the television receive-only marketplace, to underserved communities,

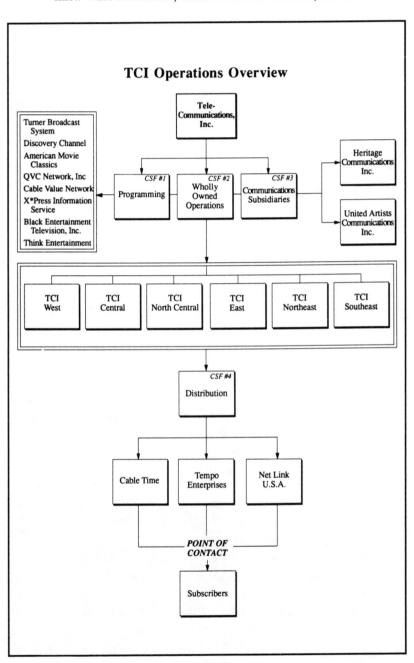

Figure 4.10

and to owners of home satellite dishes. It also transmits Superstation WTBS to cable systems nationwide.

A Membership Wholesaler   The Price Club, aptly named, was started by Sol Price and his son Robert after Sol made the worst business decision of his life. He sold 75 percent ownership of his FedMart discount stores to a West German retailer. Following major disputes with the new owner, Sol was fired as president. While unemployed, Sol and Robert took long walks. Together they hammered out a new distribution concept for small businesses. As you study the unique operations overview (Figure 4.11) of this cash-and-carry membership warehouse pioneer, remember that its limited assortment of merchandise turns over 24 times a year.

The Price Club is a public company that trades on the NAS-DAQ Exchange (symbol: PCLB) with 5,231 shareholders of record. It is staffed with 8,516 employees, one-third on a full-time basis. In its decade of hypergrowth, Price Club sales increased from $146 million to $5.0 billion.

- *Critical Success Factor 1: Membership.*
  The Price Club facilities are open only to its two million members who must present picture identification cards upon entry. Before a new warehouse is opened, The Price Club solicits area businesses through direct mail for wholesale members. Retail membership is available to federal, state, and local government employees; savings and loan, bank and credit union employees; utility, transportation, hospital, public and private school employees.
- *Critical Success Factor 2: Buying.*
  Price Club buying specialists purchase goods directly from the manufacturer. Volume discounts, prompt payment allowances, the absence of middleman costs, and tight buying controls keep gross margins under 10 percent.
- *Critical Success Factor 3: Distribution.*
  Since most distributors don't make stops for less than $500 in sales, The Price Club established itself for the small

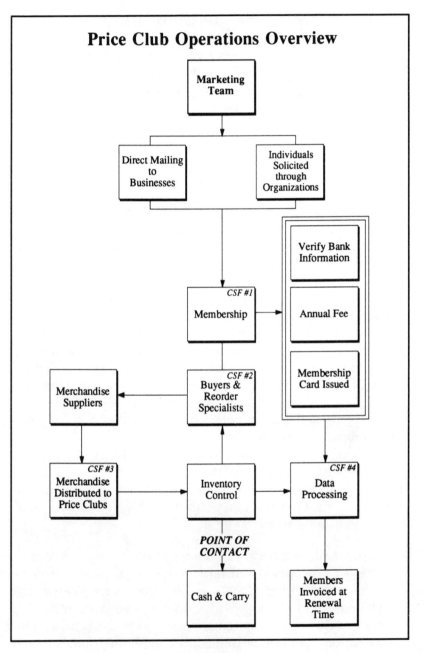

Figure 4.11

business owner who needs industrial-sized products at discount prices. Its average inventory turnover occurs every 16 days, compared to every 90 days at discount stores and twice a year at full-service retailers.

- *Critical Success Factor 4: Data Processing.*
  Data processing is used to monitor membership status, manage product inventories, and maintain tight operational controls. Computers retain detailed membership information—from business name and address to state resale permit and drivers license data.

A Telecommunications Company William McGowan was the son of a railroad organizer in the coal country of Pennsylvania. With a business degree from Harvard, McGowan raised capital to start a manufacturing company. After the venture went public, McGowan sold his interest and traveled the world. When he returned to consulting, McGowan met Jack Goekin, founder of Microwave Communications Corporation. McGowan provided Goekin with a $50,000 cash infusion in exchange for half interest in the company which he later reincorporated as MCI Communications. As you review its operating structure (Figure 4.12), remember that MCI raised more than $100 million while it had zero income, then grabbed nearly 15 percent of AT&T's market share to become the second largest long distance company in America.

MCI is a public company located in Washington, DC, that trades NASDAQ Exchange (symbol: MCIC) with 61,252 shareholders of record. It is staffed with 19,000 nonunion employees. In its decade of hypergrowth, MCI sales increased from $234 million to $6.5 billion.

- *Critical Success Factor 1: Domestic Telephone Services.*
  The MCI network transmits voice, data, facsimile, teleprinter, and other signals to and from anywhere in the United States. MCI provides operator services including collect, third-party charging, person-to-person and station-to-station operator assistance in completing domestic and international calls.

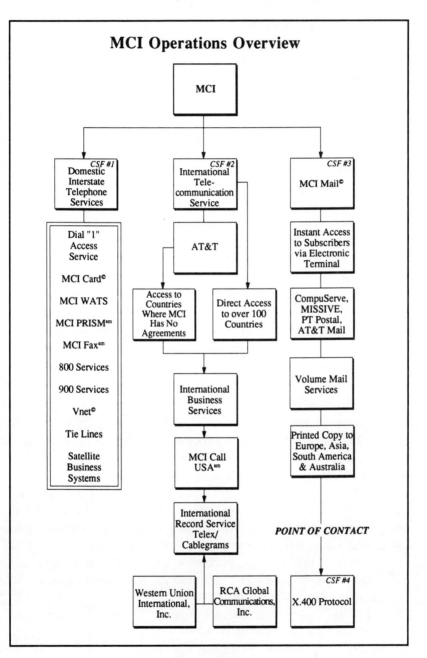

Figure 4.12

- *Critical Success Factor 2: International Telephone Service.*
  MCI offers calling to more than 100 foreign countries under its agreements with telecommunications providers in those countries. Its private leased lines provide for point-to-point transmission of overseas voice, data, and facsimile communications.

- *Critical Success Factor 3: Electronic Mail.*
  MCI Mail permits subscribers to send instant messages from virtually any electronic terminal, such as a computer, to any other electronic terminal worldwide. If the intended recipient is not an MCI subscriber, a facsimile, telex, or printed copy can be sent via independent courier or U.S. postal service.

- *Critical Success Factor 4: Protocol.*
  MCI operates within the X.400 Protocol, the standard format for international electronic communications. So subscribers of MCI mail can send and receive electronic messages to and from subscribers of Compuserve, MISSIVE, PT Postel, Sprint Mail, AT&T Mail, and other public electronic mail service providers.

An Apparel Manufacturer and Retailer   Leslie Wexner dropped out of law school to work at his parents' store, which carried his name. One day, Wexner suggested to his father that they sell only sportswear since it was the only profitable line. When his father disagreed, Wexner decided to start his own store with a $5,000 loan from an aunt. He called it The Limited. As you consider this operations overview (Figure 4.13), keep in mind that The Limited is now the world's largest specialty retailer of women's apparel.

The Limited is a public company located in Columbus, Ohio, that trades on the New York, London, and Tokyo Stock Exchanges (symbol: LTD) with 10,700 shareholders of record. It is staffed with 50,200 "associates," 60 percent on a part-time basis. In its decade of hypergrowth, The Limited's sales increased from $295 million to $4.6 billion.

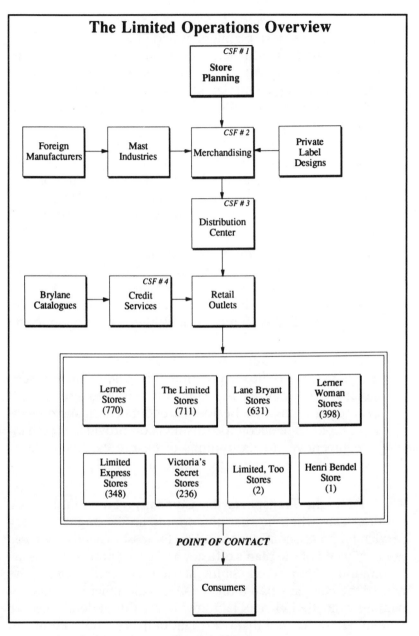

Figure 4.13

- *Critical Success Factor 1: Store Planning.*
  The Limited's store planners provide highly functional designs consistent with each division's merchandising approach. Virtually all of Wexner's stores are located in leased shopping center facilities where property landlords provide construction allowances to defray permanent improvement costs.

- *Critical Success Factor 2: Merchandising.*
  Leslie Wexner contracts with 6,800 suppliers and factories worldwide to manufacture knock-off fashions. To consolidate its merchandising, The Limited acquired Mast Industries, which serves as its primary overseas manufacturing manager.

- *Critical Success Factor 3: Distribution.*
  The Limited operates an integrated distribution system to support its retail operations. Merchandise shipped to the Columbus, Ohio, distribution facility is received, inspected, marked with retail prices, then shipped on to the designated stores.

- *Critical Success Factor 4: Credit Services.*
  The Limited Credit Corporation is a wholly owned subsidiary that finances the company's private credit card charge plan activities. Besides extending credit and collecting on past due accounts, this division provides merchandise incentives to its millions of charge card customers, such as discounts and early notification of sales.

An Air Freight Transportation Company Fred Smith was a junior at Yale when he first blueprinted an overnight delivery service for an economics paper. Yet, Professor Challis Hall was not convinced of the plan's efficacy and gave Smith a "C" for his inspiration. When Fred Smith started Federal Express, he named the company based on the speculation that he would be hauling cancelled checks nationwide for the Federal Reserve System. Smith figured that overnight delivery would eliminate the three-day time float and save The Reserve $3 million per day. Look carefully at the operations overview (Figure 4.14) and

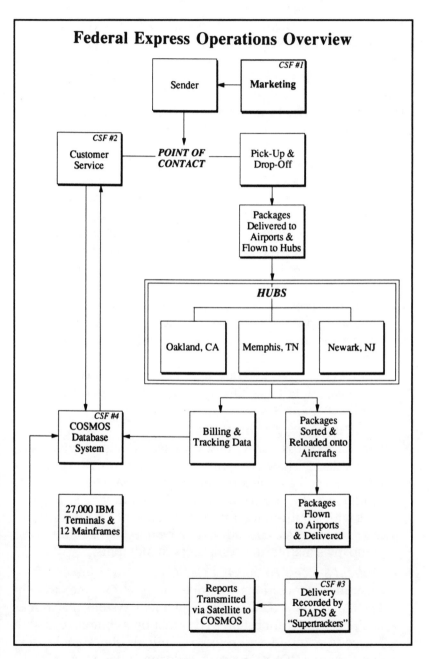

Figure 4.14

consider the information-intensity of Federal's time-definite priority package delivery business.

Federal Express Corporation is a public company that trades on the New York Stock Exchange (symbol: FDX) with 6,902 shareholders of record. It is staffed with 51,000 non-union employees worldwide. In its decade of hypergrowth, Federal Express sales increased from $415 million to $5.2 billion.

- *Critical Success Factor 1: Marketing.*
  The marketing of Federal Express, which emphasizes the strategic value of overnight distribution, helped manufacturers, restaurants, and specialty stores, and leverage overnight value-added delivery as a primary element of their differentiation strategies. Its TV commercials were so popular that the words, "Hello-o-o-o Federal!" became part of American folklore.

- *Critical Success Factor 2: Customer Service.*
  Federal Express guarantees service to 98 percent of the population in 40,000 counties of America's 335 major markets. Highly trained agents at 14 decentralized service centers receive up to 200,000 telephone calls daily and book pick-ups, quote rates, direct couriers, figure discounts, and profile customers.

- *Critical Success Factor 3: DADS.*
  Federal Express has 17,000 vehicles equipped with Digitally Aided Dispatch Systems (DADS) that provide couriers with dispatch and pick-up information. DADS incorporates "SuperTracker" bar code readers that let drivers scan packages with a built-in light-pen. The relevant data is transmitted to local offices by radio, then beamed by satellite to the company's mainframe computers in Memphis.

- *Critical Success Factor 4: COSMOS.*
  Customer Operations Service Master On-line System (COSMOS) is a database management system that tracks each package from origin to destination as employees with bar-code scanners and remote terminals check each package through COSMOS up to a dozen times in its travels. Real-time monitoring traces package information for call-in

customers, minimizes routing mistakes, and helps drivers spot delinquent accounts.

A Discount Merchandiser   Sam Walton began his career as a management trainee with the J.C. Penney Company. He then joined the Ben Franklin chain in Newport, Arkansas. After five years, the landlord would not renew Walton's lease. So he moved to Bentonville, Arkansas, and started over. When Walton saw new competition on the horizon in the form of discounting, he opened the first Wal-Mart Discount City in Rogers, Arkansas. Don't be fooled by the simplicity of its operations overview (Figure 4.15) because Wal-Mart offers more than 70,000 different name-brand items at everyday low prices through its 1,200 stores for one-stop family shopping.

Wal-Mart is a public company located in Bentonville, Arkansas, that trades on the New York and Pacific Stock Exchanges (symbol: WMT) with 80,175 shareholders of record. It is staffed with 275,000 "associates." In its decade of hypergrowth, Wal-Mart sales increased from $1.6 billion to $25.8 billion.

- *Critical Success Factor 1: Purchasing.*
  While Wal-Mart maintains centralized buying practices, its regional merchandising system customizes purchases based on 128 traits such as climate, ethnic orientation, and recreational preferences. More than 100,000 manufacturer's reps form the heart of Wal-Mart's merchandise supply line.
- *Critical Success Factor 2: Distribution.*
  Wal-Mart's warehouse distribution centers service 175 stores in a six-hour driving radius to insure daily product deliveries. These high-tech distribution centers utilize online order receipt from store registers, online reordering from vendors, and automatic inventory control.
- *Critical Success Factor 3: Marketing.*
  Wal-Mart's marketing is rooted in the belief that once customers try the store they will always return. Walton's print advertising consists of monthly circulars and television to boost Wal-Mart's image on a market-by-market basis. Its

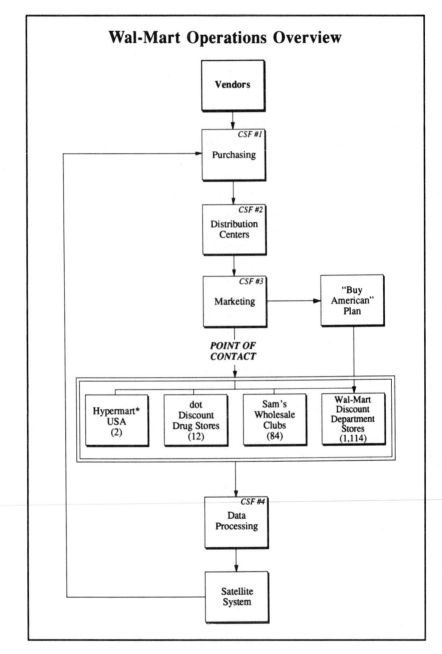

Figure 4.15

"greeter program" consists of senior citizens who welcome Wal-Mart customers, place stickers on return packages, and guide them to the exchange desk.

- *Critical Success Factor 4: Data Processing.*
Wal-Mart's data communications technology is part of a sophisticated network that integrates each store's mini-computer with the home office mainframe. A $20 million satellite communications system provides real-time, around-the-clock transmission of voice, picture, and computer data.

PULL IT ALL TOGETHER

Knowing what you do best, then doing it better than anyone else can be graphically depicted through your operations overview. A simple flow chart that identifies your critical success factors can position your company for hypergrowth. From there, support data can be generated, emerging opportunities pinpointed, and conclusions about future directions discussed. Designing your operations overview provides insights about how your company should function when all the pieces fit together.

Once the operations overview fixes accountability, feedback mechanisms can link strategy to tactics. The operations overview establishes your organizational framework. The more this framework is communicated, the more likely it will become internalized by your entire organization.

The operations overview improves your organizational design and clarifies reporting relationships. Finally, the foundation for your managerial system ties detailed job descriptions to the operations overview.

Development of the operations overview requires active involvement from your executive team. Managers who commit to this exercise achieve maximum effectiveness as all business activities become syncronized. The operations overview serves as a point of reference for managerial thought and action as it adjusts to the dynamic environment of hypergrowth.

II

Make It
Happen

In business there are
Those who make it happen
Those who watch it happen
and
Those who ask, "What's happening?"

To achieve Hypergrowth, you have to make it happen!

5

Give 'Em What They Really Want
(Not What You Think
They Should Want)

A fundamental principle of marketing says "give people what they really want, not what you think they should want." More often than not, executives try to anticipate what their customers should want, instead of listening to what they really want. Hypergrowth just doesn't work that way. You can have the best designed and best managed operation under the sun. But never forget that you don't conduct business in a vacuum. To discover what your customers really want, invest in research:

- *Grassroots research.*
  Reebok spotted emerging athletic trends at the grassroots where fun and word-of-mouth advertising build awareness. Unable to afford extensive research, Reebok sent employees to aerobics classes in church basements to demonstrate the value of its shoes. Instructors who wore ballet shoes, running shoes, or nothing at all had the injuries to show for it. They became quick converts and credible demonstrators of Reebok footwear.

- *Community research.*
  Wal-Mart developed a regional merchandising system through Computer Aided Design (CAD). This system tailored merchandise offerings to the needs of individual store communities. It monitors 128 regional traits including climate, rural/urban, military, college, industrial, retirement mix, and much more. This information helps Wal-Mart plan stores, customize inventory, control distribution, and improve sales.

- *Demographic research.*
  Home Depot conducts extensive research by tracking thousands of do-it-yourself customers. Its demographic profiles dictate where to open multiple stores. Its stores are tailored to the white collar, urban professional population in well-established transporation hubs where home ownership exceeds 70 percent and family income surpasses $35,000.

- *Market research.*
  Compaq conducts extensive market research of its dealers, customers, and designers, then converts its findings into new product ideas. Compaq views itself as a marketing company that provides business solutions. Its research helps establish a clear corporate mission based on customer needs. Once Compaq uncovers real needs, it creates technologies to satisfy those needs.

- *Industry research.*
  Federal Express research revealed that many industrial customers could not afford to duplicate inventories warehoused around the country. It then targeted the top 37,000 businesses located in the 100 leading U.S. metropolitan markets, which accounted for 84 percent of all domestic air shipments. Its industry research also revealed that the Postal Service handled 200 million pieces of certified, registered, special delivery, and express mail annually. As a result of its research, Federal Express supplemented its package deliveries with express letters in its overnight infrastructure.

Once your research is completed, be sure to give customers what they really want, not what you think they should want. Research into the core values of today's marketplace reveals what customers really want: guarantees, superior service, value, state-of-the art design, education and training, function and fashion, low prices, and community service.

GUARANTEE PEACE OF MIND

Hypergrowth can occur when you provide a pleasant and friendly buying experience. Consider offering a "Satisfaction Guaranteed" refund and exchange policy. This is why Wal-Mart customers are confident when purchasing its merchandise. Like Wal-Mart, The Limited offers a "no sale is ever final" guarantee. If at anytime a customer is not satisfied, they simply return the merchandise with their receipt for a credit, refund, or exchange . . . no questions asked.

Get Creative

Reebok management learned that creative risk-taking pays off. With the introduction of its first tennis shoe, Reebok offered this unique guarantee: the most comfortable tennis shoe ever worn or Reebok would refund the unhappy consumer's money accompanied by a free can of tennis balls. The risk paid off as Reebok sold millions of shoes and sent out only 128 cans of tennis balls.

Put Up or Shut Up

Federal Express realized that its customers didn't care about speed, price, or logistics. What customers really wanted from their overnight delivery service was *peace of mind.*

So 12 times during its journey, from pick-up to delivery, each package gets scanned. The data is sent to a central computer at the company's Memphis office. When a customer dials a toll-free number, the operator tells them the exact location of the package. If Federal Express can't locate a package within 30 minutes, the customer doesn't pay. Federal Express then went one step further. If its Priority One packages arrive after 10:30 A.M., the customer again doesn't pay. This became the thrust of its advertising: "Federal Express—When It Absolutely, Positively, Has To Be There Overnight." Delivering peace of mind became a permanent part of its corporate positioning statement.

PROVIDE SUPERIOR SERVICE

Superior service assumes that the sale marks the beginning of a long-term relationship. When you treat your customers as the most important people in your company, they will purchase other products from you. Superior service provides the opportunity to resell satisfied customers again in the future.

Offer a Test Drive

Apple Computer offered an innovative approach to the standard product demonstration: sample loaners. In its fourth year of hypergrowth, Apple purchased every advertising page in a special post-election issue of *Newsweek* magazine. The issue's fold-out ad read, "Test Drive a Macintosh." More than 200,000 people took a Macintosh home for a free 24-hour trial.

Over the years, Apple has provided many variations on its test drive theme including demo kits, limited version software, and sample packages. This let customers try new products, which made the purchase decision easier.

Go Out of Your Way to Be Helpful

TCI's mission is to bring quality service to its cable customers. They go out of their way to help underserved communities and owners of home satellite dishes. TCI also works closely with its broadcasters, cable programmers, and local governments in order to provide the best possible service to its most important asset—the customer.

Make It Easy

The Price Club provides immediate product availability as buyers pick the merchandise from the warehouse floor and carry it to their cars. Customers can try new products without a large inventory investment. The Price Club stays open seven days a week with additional hours for its wholesale members.

Give Around-the-Clock Service

Leslie Wexner likes to provide around-the-clock service for his catalog division. The Limited trains up a knowledgable staff of associates who respond quickly to customer needs by phone, 24 hours a day. The most important value at The Limited is to offer the absolute best customer shopping experience anywhere. This is based on Wexner's philosophy of "the customer first, last, and always."

Improve Accessibility

No detail is too small to escape the Home Depot's attention. For example, store opening hours were adjusted to better serve the professional wanting to purchase supplies before arriving at the job site. Bernard Marcus also trained specialized sales staff to handle the professional's job orders. The Home Depot also employs professional tradesmen at each location to provide customer assistance throughout a complex project.

Prior to selecting individual store sites, planners obtain detailed market studies that indicate growth prospects for market areas. Home Depot then targets store locations for major commercial thoroughfares that are accessible to both established neighborhoods and new residential developments.

Eliminate Delays

To achieve better service, Sam Walton tries to eliminate delays. Wal-Mart's point-of-sale technology, for example, reduced bank card approval response time from 30 seconds to only 6 seconds. From the location of a layaway desk to the installation of a sorting system, Wal-Mart has but one objective—improve service to its customers. Wal-Mart also features overhead "no wait rebate" signs for discounts on small electrics, stackout cubes for beauty aids, and promotional tables in aisles for best values.

Enhance Your Service

Consumers no longer tolerate inefficiency or inflexibility when they have other options. Federal Express was keenly aware of this and worked to provide ever-better value to its customers. The key to its success has been the ability to provide individual solutions to its customers' future needs.

Federal Express realized that its customers were not professional shipping agents, but secretaries and executives who knew little about air freight. So they looked for ways to improve service through unique value-added benefits.

Each service agent with a computer can tell new customers the detailed location of the nearest drop box. This information is displayed on the computer screen and relayed in simple terms like "go into the hotel lobby, turn left and the Federal Express box is at the far end near the check-out desk."

Federal Express customers only care about solutions to their business problems. When customers needed a better way to store and deliver inventories, Federal Express turned its Memphis headquarters into a giant warehouse to stockpile supplies for scores of its commercial customers. From this "parts bank," companies dispatch products wherever they are needed and consequently lowered their inventory costs.

Provide Technical Support

Computer Associates (CA) provides technical support to cover the entire span of its products. With all levels of support and development working closely together, CA touts the best technical support in the industry.

CA improved support through increased training and telephone contact with clients. They expanded hours during which telephone support was available. Charles Wang also introduced CA-UNISERVICE/II, an enhanced version of CA's online service, support, and training system.

DELIVER VALUE

You want your customers to receive full value from your products and services. Delivering value means that each customer experience with your company is a satisfying one. Realize that everybody in your company can be fired by your customers if they choose to shop elsewhere. Every concept perceived, every technology developed and every associate employed should be directed with this one objective clearly in mind—deliver full value to your customers.

Provide Quality Merchandise at Low Prices

Sam Walton built his Wal-Mart empire on quality, name-brand merchandise offered at everyday low prices. Walton's promise of the lowest prices lets customers shop without waiting for sales. The combination of low prices and a broad selection of quality merchandise gives shoppers genuine value. Although Wal-Mart keeps tight control over expenses, its low prices are keyed by volume and timing. Wal-Mart purchases tonnage close to the start and end of each buying season when manufacturers unload products at their lowest prices.

Wal-Mart adopted operational lessons from Sam's Wholesale Club, such as premarking, palletization, and commodity packaging to push its prices even lower. Moving merchandise mechanically rather than manually also brought Wal-Mart new breakthroughs in efficiency.

Wal-Mart's small-town strategy and Sam's Warehouse Club metro efforts are both predicated on selling high quality name-brand merchandise at the lowest possible price. Walton's drive to deliver value may even be recession-proof since Wal-Mart sales increased by 42 and 44 percent during the last two recessions.

Help Save Time and Money

Liz Claiborne's success was an outgrowth of her philosophy to offer designer clothes at nondesigner prices. For years, the monied class dictated fashion design. Liz Claiborne set out to help the middle-class woman look as smart as the wealthy. With millions of women entering the service sector, she discovered a huge unfilled niche: stylish clothes for working women.

Claiborne created "color-by-the-numbers" fashion to save working women time and money. Most items in Claiborne's sportswear collection are sold as "separates" rather than ensembles, such as suits. Claiborne's separates, dresses, and related accessory designs have replaced drab workwear with color and comfort. Designs are mixed and matched in stores. Related styles, fabrics, and colors are displayed over extended periods so wardrobes can be coordinated from season to season.

Liz Claiborne's designer clothes maintain consumer recognition across product lines. When pricing her clothes, Liz assumes the attitude of her customers. She asks herself, "How much would I be willing to pay for that piece?" To keep prices low, Claiborne contracts with independent foreign suppliers. Savings in labor costs are passed on to the consumer in the form of nondesigner prices.

Liz Claiborne tries to offer the best in fashion value in business and leisure wear. While most dress makers concentrate on either inexpensive "wrapper" dresses or expensive fashion styles, Liz Claiborne fills the void in the middle. Her style and sourcing capabilities are perfectly suited for this fashion niche.

Finally, to help save time and provide the model of value for the fashion industry, Liz Claiborne opened a small chain of retail stores called First Issue. These shops sell only Claiborne merchandise, which makes it easier to broaden product lines and fulfill the Claiborne mission of offering the best value in women's fashion.

BECOME STATE-OF-THE-ART

To create your own hypergrowth opportunity, identify problems that face your customers. Then create the best combination of products, technologies, and services to solve these problems. This is how Compaq achieved the highest new product success rate in the computer industry. Compaq treats suppliers and dealers as part of its team. By certifying vendors that meet its stiff performance requirements, Compaq not only reduced costly inspection time, but forged a sense of mutual cooperation.

Design Defect-Free Products

Compaq's philosophy is to prevent problems altogether by designing it right the first time. Its defect-free products required a sophisticated quality control system that could detect failures throughout the manufacturing process. Its defect-free program saved time and money as components went directly to the assembly line without pretesting.

Compaq adheres to a basic manufacturing formula: Design the right product, then get it to market quickly. Its manufacturing operations meet the strictest quality standards as defects are not tolerated from its products.

Compaq lets the market specify the computer functions, then its engineers design them as small as possible. Compaq's defect-free breakthroughs improved utility, lowered manufacturing costs, and accelerated product development: Proprietary read-only memory (ROM) manipulates operating systems so Compaq computers run virtually all IBM software; ASIC (applications-specific integrated circuits) chips package the work of scores of integrated circuits into a single chip; reverse engineering recreates the electronic circuits and software functions of IBM personal computers.

Create New Standards

Of the factors that impact the computer's overall performance, the hard disk drive is second only to system clock speed. As databases, desktop publishing, and spreadsheets grew in size and complexity, hard disk drives became standard equipment in new computers.

Alan Shugart knew that transferring large amounts of data onto a disk for storage would require a new hard drive system. So he created an affordable 5 1/4-inch higher-capacity hard disk drive for personal computers. When IBM announced that its Personal System/2 computer would contain hard disk drives, Seagate won the $200 million IBM contract. Seagate created the hard disk drive standard, and soon became the low-cost producer of this state-of-the-art product. As a result, Seagate won half the world's market share in personal computer disk drives.

Market Your Own Products

Integrated Resources became known for professional and diversified asset management. As a hybrid—financial products manufacturer and financial products marketer—Integrated Resources adapted itself to changing investor needs. Its flexible management structure designed and marketed products that helped clients achieve top investment returns.

Integrated Resources started out as a syndicator of limited partnerships in real estate, energy, and leasing. When legislation dried up the demand for such shelters, investors diversified their portfolios. Selig Zises eliminated investor tax shelters and marketed universal life insurance, variable annuities, mutual funds, and income partnerships.

Integrated's professional money management skills fit the needs of investors wanting to diversify their portfolios for a Post-Tax-Reform, Post-Market-Crash investment environment. Diversified asset management provided a refuge for investors who could no longer deduct passive losses from limited partnership investments.

In place of its deep real estate tax shelters, Integrated Resources created and marketed a line of public real estate partnerships that were long on cash profits and short on write offs. Selig Zises quickly adapted to a new financial environment with life insurance that offered his policy holders important financial planning benefits such as tax deferral and capital growth at market interest rates. By rapidly shifting its focus to financial services, Integrated's total capital grew 41 percent, its stock price doubled, and its sales surpassed $1 billion.

Understand Technology and Resource Allocation

After winning its antitrust case with AT&T, MCI had a net worth of negative $40 million, owed the bank $100 million and had accumulated losses of $120 million. However, Bill McGowan knew that to survive, then achieve hypergrowth, MCI needed its own microwave system. Instead of leasing capacity from AT&T, McGowan designed a multi-billion dollar state-of-the-art telephone network.

Investing back into technology, McGowan expanded MCI's distribution capacity, increased revenues, and paved the way for world-wide expansion. Integration of its state-of-the-art technologies encompassed fiber optics, satellite transmission, and cellular radio.

Bill McGowan understood more than just the regulatory environment of his industry. He knew how microwave networks operated and how local phone companies interconnected. He also lived the complicated system of tariffs. Most important, McGowan knew where to focus his company's resources at every moment, even while his company bled red ink.

PROVIDE EDUCATION AND TRAINING

To build hypergrowth momentum on a national scale requires education and training. Education creates awareness and stimulates action. Training focuses on the skills needed to use a product or service. Education precedes training and provides information about the benefits of your offering. Finally, education provides meaning in the market for your hypergrowth anomaly.

Start at the Grassroots

Reebok provides grassroots support for the sports served by its products. They publish newsletters, lead injury prevention research, and sponsor seminars. Reebok formed its instructor alliances and offered aerobics teachers special deals on shoes. Paul Fireman's marketing tactics worked well as students mimicked their mentors' footwear. Reebok sponsored the first certification program for aerobics instructors and underwrote studies of aerobics-induced injuries.

Fireman then established grassroots support for walking when he invested $1 million in the Rockport Walking Institute, a gait research facility; published a book entitled *Fitness Walking* by cross-country walker, Rob Sweetgall; produced walking documentaries and sponsored walking events.

Establish Continuity

Liz Claiborne provided retailers with "Claiboard Receiving Guides." These booklets listed the names and style numbers of every item in the Claiborne line. Claiboards served as the road map to coordinating Claiborne lines. After its first booklets fell into the hands of competitors, Claiborne restricted the use of pictures to internal use only.

Train and Retrain Employees

Bernard Marcus believes in training, then retraining his Home Depot employees. Marcus personally trained each of his 118 store managers and 590 assistant managers. What distinguishes Home Depot from the competition is its approach toward training at all levels.

Marcus's six-day manager training course is an elaborate education program that transfers Home Depot's values to new management teams. Conducted eight times a year, topics include The Home Depot Mission, Profit Planning, People Management, Time Management, Management Information Systems, Delegation Skills, and Personal Productivity.

Store-level employees also receive intensive training in

weekly "product-knowledge" seminars. While paid for their time, attendance is mandatory. These classes are conducted by fellow workers and impart product information in the context of a total home improvement project. This training reinforces the importance of purchasing all products necessary to finish a job. Classes are offered in wallpapering, wiring, plumbing, carpentry, and more. Also, the Home Depot salespeople respond to customer questions at any point during a project, either on the sales floor or by telephone.

At Home Depot, the number one criterion for training is to increase sales. Store managers are taught to move as much product as possible and let merchandisers worry about maintaining the inventory.

INTEGRATE FUNCTION AND FASHION

Product breakthroughs occur when you place different variables into new combinations, then watch which ones the market chooses. This was the case when Paul Fireman set out to create the first designer athletic shoe. Reebok merged function and fashion when it placed flashy colors on durable aerobics shoes that felt like slippers. Sporting goods retailers couldn't keep Reeboks on the shelves.

Become Market-Driven

Reebok management recognizes that it is first and foremost a consumer marketing company. Its foundation for success is a superior ability to understand the constantly changing demands of its customers.

Reebok is a market-driven rather than a product-driven company. Not married to one style or one activity, Reebok designs shoes for specific lifestyles. This focus led Paul Fireman into emerging growth markets with new categories of products. When consumers demanded footwear for a new sport, Reebok responded with shoes unparalleled in comfort, performance, and style.

At Reebok, production does not start until a shoe offers specific design, technology, or functional advantages. Once a shoe proves superior to its competiton, Reebok manufactures it quickly, then distributes it through quality retailers.

Paul Fireman stays close to his trend-setting consumers, since they demand new styles every few months. These core consumers dictate new shoe features and benefits. Reebok then blends fashion and function to meet their comfort and durability needs. Fireman knows that consumers dictate Reebok's growth rate, since they are its ultimate purchasing agent.

Paul Fireman relinquished his presidency to complete Reebok's shift from an entrepreneurial phenom into a mature industry leader. While he remained spokesperson to the financial community, Fireman returned to his true passion—the shoe itself. He then recruited a new president, senior vice-president of marketing, and a U.S. division president. However, within two years, Fireman took back day-to-day control when he fired his upper management staff. Fireman built a new management team and put them on the road to win back lost retailers and revive Reebok's entrepreneurial spirit.

Move Faster Than Your Competition

Fashion originality was never a priority at The Limited. Instead, Leslie Wexner's genius resides in his conceptual retooling of the retail mechanics. Wexner built The Limited on interlocking strategies: Ride emerging clothing trends with low-cost, knock-off sportswear. Then, with centralized distribution, deliver this sportswear quickly through a galaxy of stores.

Leslie Wexner is simply a "fast second," once a fashion trend has been established. He tracks new fashions and creates low-priced, private label copies for his customers, faster than his competition. Leslie Wexner is not as interested in fashion as he is in the business of fashion. So he actually puts a higher priority on the marketing of clothes than on their creation.

The Limited's strength is its execution. In Wexner's action culture, he pondors, experiments, then rolls out. For example, he considered a lingerie concept for three years, then acquired

Victoria's Secret as a way to test his formula. Once the formula succeeded, Wexner opened 250 lingerie stores in just 36 months.

Wexner plans to dominate the $50 billion-a-year women's clothing business by overtaking department stores. These "dinosaurs," as he refers to them, sell 40 percent of women's clothes and survive due to real estate acquired long ago. Wexner shuns their traditional marketing tools such as surveys, focus groups, and advertising, which he regards as "crutches" used by retailers who do not have a "feel" for fashion.

OFFER LOW PRICES

Low prices can turn lookers into buyers. At Wal-Mart, a "shelf talker" under oil filters reads, "In order to maintain our low everyday pricing, we will not be individually ticketing items in this section." Low prices also inspired Bill McGowan to take on the entrenched telephone company. McGowan figured MCI could offer up to a 50 percent discount on long distance telephone calls. While some companies use low prices as a loss leader, other companies make low prices the focus of their business.

Stimulate New Business

John Malone cut prices on TCI's cable service as part of a special promotion. New subscribers were offered pay service for only $2 a month until year's end. While the number of full-price pay subscribers dropped, the volume of the $2 units sold as part of the promotion more than compensated for the difference. Following the promotion, TCI converted a large number of the 750,000 new customers into full-priced subscribers.

Lose Sales Intelligently

The Price Club specializes in offering low prices. Known as "the intelligent loss of sales," this innovative approach to mass merchandising did not emerge from detailed research or great marketing. Instead Sol and Robert Price simply mark products as cheaply as possible. Then they purposely "lose sales" to achieve higher volumes and faster turnover.

For example, retailers offer pickles in several sizes: $1.99 small, $2.99 medium, and $3.99 large. When considering its inventory, The Price Club figured no sales would be lost if the $1.99 size was eliminated. Management then projected that one out of ten sales would be lost if the $2.99 size was dropped. So in losing one customer, the nine remaining customers would purchase the $3.99 size.

The intelligent loss of sales also drives up the average purchase price with larger sizes and multiple quantities. Rather than selling video cassettes one at a time, The Price Club offers them only in packs of ten. And while most retailers sell quarts of mayonnaise, The Price Club offers it only by the gallon.

The Price Club specializes in bargains. While department stores sell items with an average margin of 50 percent, discount stores 30 percent, food retailers 20 percent, The Price Club merchandise is sold at an average margin of under 10 percent.

For its merchandise to be sold at such low mark-ups, overhead costs such as credit cards, decor, private labels, advertising, and deliveries had to be eliminated. The Price Club also avoids lease agreements based on a percentage of sales. In most cases, the land under its warehouses is purchased. The intelligent loss of sales even extends to shareholders. The company does not pay a cash dividend since it would be taxed once as corporate income and again as personal income of shareholders.

Give Volume Discounts

Businessland's phenomenal growth was due to its discounted prices and strong support services. When the local area network (LAN) wave hit, Businessland helped corporate customers who couldn't solve the LAN complexities on their own. Then it sold thousands of personal computers at volume discounts to large corporate customers.

PROVIDE COMMUNITY SERVICE

As part of your hypergrowth success, you will be asked to meet needs on a community level. Develop long-term partnerships with those who make up the communities you serve. Publicity and sales will take a back seat to meeting community needs. This occurred when Liz Claiborne retired from the fashion industry, then channeled all of her energies into environmental causes.

Identify with the Needs

To help out the inner city youth, Reebok renovated worn-out inner city basketball courts, then gave samples of its newly designed basketball shoes to a "core" group of trend setters. Reebok knew that while its 15- to 22-year-old consumers constituted only 15 percent of the U.S. population, they buy 30 percent of the sneakers and influence another 10 percent of the sales by example. Reebok also reached high school and college consumers by underwriting a series of rock concerts to raise money for a human rights organization.

Provide Scholarships

The "Community Involvement" program is Sam Walton's corporate commitment to the communities Wal-Mart serves. Each local store presents annual scholarships to deserving area high school seniors. More than $1 million in scholarships are awarded each year by the Wal-Mart chain. The Wal-Mart Foundation also provides matching fund grants to meet other needs of local communities.

Start a Philanthropy Program

While Reebok became the first shoe company to create a philanthropic foundation, Integrated Resources started its Philanthropic Financial Services program, whereby donated assets are placed in a charitable remainder trust and reinvested for economic and tax advantages. The benefits are shared by the investor, corporation, and charities alike.

Create New Jobs

Wal-Mart initiated the "Buy American" program as a cooperative effort between retailers and domestic manufacturers to re-establish a competitive position for American-made goods. Sam Walton expressed his views in a message to his vendors, "Find products that American manufacturers have stopped producing because they couldn't compete with foreign imports."

The goal of this program was to create more jobs and reduce the trade deficit. It converted more than $1 billion in retail purchases, which meant that nearly 18,000 manufacturing jobs and 30,000 service positions were retained for Americans. This was based on Department of Commerce statistics that equated each $1 million of lost merchandise production to 223 jobs.

Thank Those Who've Helped You

Leslie Wexner, founder of The Limited, gave the largest individual contribution ever to his alma mater, Ohio State University. His $15 million gift, accompanied by $10 million in previous donations to the Wexner Center for the Visual Arts, insured that the center would be built according to its award-winning design.

Wexner gives money to other causes such as the United Way, the Downtown Columbus Renovation Project, and the Boy Scouts. Wexner also gives $1 million a year to the United Jewish Appeal.

Teach a Man to Fish

Sol Price lives out the adage, "Give a man a fish and you feed him for a day. Teach a man to fish and you feed him for a lifetime." When Price retired from The Price Club, he donated $3.5 million for a combined retail school and nonprofit discount store. The San Diego School of Retailing enrolls young adults and teaches them progressive methods of retailing. The adjourning 48,000-square-foot Gateway Marketplace provides hands-on experience of the principles taught in school.

Find a Need and Fill It

Few companies have focused as much on community service as Apple Computer. And few companies have experienced as much success as Apple Computer. Yet, most of Apple's community service programs focus on education: Apple gave more than 10,000 Apple II computers to schools as part of the "Kids Can't Wait" program; Apple sponsored Computer Club competitions; Apple offered computer training scholarships for school educators; Apple gave educators special computer rebates through its "Apple for the Teacher" program; Apple introduced "Apple Unified School System" and its "Education Purchase" program to integrate computers into the learning process; Apple awarded more than $1 million in computer grants for its "Equal Time" program that helped students develop higher thinking skills.

Apple's Community Affairs division also awarded grants to civic groups that dealt with issues such as housing, drug abuse, the environment, employment, medical research, the arts, youth, and the elderly; Apple's Employee Volunteer Action program matched the skills of Apple employees with community needs; Apple also installed Macintosh computers in 100 Ronald McDonald Houses across the country. Helping the community helped Apple develop goodwill and word-of-mouth advertising for its products.

HOW TO GIVE 'EM WHAT THEY REALLY WANT

Hypergrowth requires tremendous foresight and planning to acquire and allocate the resources needed to fuel a fast-growing venture in a rapidly changing environment. Before you invest your first dollar in manufacturing or marketing, determine the potential size of your market. Then project how fast you'll grow. Finally, figure out how you'll make good on your commitments.

Calculate Your Market's Potential

With hypergrowth, you don't always know the market potential for a product or service. The walking shoe market, for example, emerged from its geriatric and orthopedic roots to become one of the largest segments of the entire athletic footwear industry. Reebok helped expand the walking market to 55 million Americans, from strollers to speed walkers. The walking market now buys 125 million pairs of shoes annually with total sales of $3 billion.

Reebok introduced technically advanced features such as a "toe box" with extra room, super-absorbent lining, and a flexible curved sole to facilitate rocking motions. By developing a true walking shoe, Reebok established walking both as a sport and a fitness exercise rather than just a commonplace activity. Walkers soon outnumbered joggers 2 to 1 as 6,500 walking clubs promoted the activity.

Develop Predictive Models

Federal Express climbed to its leadership position by convincing customers that its service could mean the difference between success and failure. Incisive package volume prediction models calculated Federal's hypergrowth. Fred Smith designed the "Air Express Buying Power Index" to measure his penetration within major air freight markets. This index correlated the Standard Industrial Classification (SIC) codes with actual use of air freight by companies in those industries. Smith then developed a database of companies that represented major prospects for overnight shipping of time-sensitive, high priority packages.

Ratios for expected package volume per employee in each category were established. These ratios were then matched with SIC employment figures and its Buying Power Index for each metropolitan area. The predictive model helped calculate

Federal's market share and establish budgets for national sales, promotion, and advertising expenditures.

Deliver Steak, Not Just the Sizzle

Compaq designed products that improved productivity. Gadgets and "gee whiz" technology took a back seat to IBM-compatibility and top performance. While IBM moved customers to more expensive machines for more power, Compaq allowed its customers to upgrade older machines as their needs changed. Compaq's portable and desktop models avoided the high-tech glitz. Instead, they figured out what was strategically important and built it into their products.

6

Take Charge!

C EOs don't build a billion-dollar enterprise in a vacuum. It requires people working with and through others to accomplish the "impossible." Hypergrowth requires much more than just managing ideas or products. Hypergrowth CEOs are responsible for the corporate image, research, employees, managers, customers, competitors, networks, costs, cash flow, margins, assets, technology, suppliers, bureaucrats, and manufacturers.

A particular CEO, like any other human being, has strengths, weaknesses, and areas of greater or lesser capability. He or she has an individual style, prioritizes differently, may tend to focus on the big picture or be very detail-oriented. CEOs must communicate a dynamic vision and develop a personal and organizational modus operandi capable of creating and sustaining hypergrowth.

BUILD A SMART TEAM

With so many demands placed on the visionary, hypergrowth has introduced a new management dynamic called the "smart team." Hypergrowth executives know that putting the right management team in place from the start is imperative for success. Many venture capitalists, in fact, walk away from

117

opportunities if a strong management team is not present when they are ready to invest.

The smart team concept is an interdisciplinary approach to management whereby critical decisions are made by consensus. It assumes that a marketing vice-president and a chief financial officer can provide valuable input regarding a distribution decision.

The development of a strong management team is a top priority in building a hypergrowth company. Smart team leaders orchestrate their corporate activities to tap the full potential of each team member. Like the coxswain of a rowing team, they strive to keep each member pulling together.

The smart team process involves informal meetings where participants discuss projections, problems, and policies. Every department involved gives its view. Then the group separates the key issues, examines the trade-offs, and arrives at a consensus decision.

Smart team success requires participants to follow basic guidelines. First, smart teams integrate the components of hypergrowth success: the right marketing strategy, the right product strategy, the right management structure, the right execution, and the right financial resources. Next, the spirit of the process implies that if anybody on the team isn't satisfied, the decision does not proceed until that member learns what others know or they convince the team the other way. Finally, to keep up with the breakneck rate of change, management must keep a fluid organizational structure that evolves to meet hypergrowth's demands.

Hypergrowth smart teams display an unusual management dynamic. They are especially tolerant of each other since they share the responsibility for making the process work. As you put your smart team in place, consider how others made it work. Several CEOs made smart teams a key factor in their success.

Visualize a Large Company in Its Formative Stage

When Rod Canion, Jim Harris, and Bill Murto quit their jobs at Texas Instruments, they had worked together a combined total of 34 years. Canion was a manager, Harris an engineer, and Murto a marketing analyst. From the start, they hired people who could manage a billion-dollar company. They always considered Compaq a large company in its formative stages, rather than a small company that would grow large.

Compaq's smart team recruited other seasoned professionals with generous salaries and stock options. John Gribi joined the smart team as CFO and set up Compaq's state-of-the-art accounting system. Next, John Walker, a senior vice-president at Data Point, was recruited to establish a top-quality manufacturing operation. Then Sparky Sparks, a 20-year IBM sales veteran, was brought on to crack the dealer network. The behind-the-scenes member of the smart team was Ben Rosen, Chairman of the Board at Compaq.

Pick the Right Players from the Start

Liz Claiborne's smart team was comprised of four key players whose combined strengths fueled hypergrowth. From day one, Liz complimented her skills in design with Arthur Ortenberg's skills in finance and administration, Jerome Chazen's skills in sales and marketing, and Leonard Boxer's skills in production and sourcing. Together they manufactured and distributed fashionable, functional, and affordable apparel for the working woman.

Establish Unity of Purpose

Known for its depth of management, the Integrated Resources smart team was comprised of boyhood chums. Selig Zises, Jay Zises, and Arthur Goldberg not only grew up in the same neighborhood, they remained partners for nearly two decades after starting their company.

Never Fear Failure

Bernard Marcus and co-founder Arthur Blank needed a merchandising executive to help launch the Home Depot. They approached Pat Farrah who had just declared bankruptcy in a retail venture that prefigured Home Depot's store operation. Marcus and Blank liked Farrah's concept and made him a partner in the Home Depot start-up.

Know Your Roles

Computer Associates was founded by Charles Wang (marketing), Russell Artzt (customer support and product development), Judith Cedeno (finance), and Bill Habermaas (product development) who stayed together through the entire hypergrowth decade. This smart team bartered computer time and programming in exchange for their first office space.

Challenge Your Smart Team

The Price Club was founded by Sol Price and his smart team of Robert Price (President), Giles Bateman (CFO), and Richard Libenson (COO) who stayed together from inception through the end of their hypergrowth decade. Sol kept the intensity high by challenging his team to stay ahead of the marketplace. They went on to pioneer the $25 billion membership warehouse industry.

Once your smart team is in place, prepare to manage the many facets of your hypergrowth venture.

MANAGE YOUR IMAGE

Your company's image can be carefully engineered and adapted to meet the challenges of a competitive marketplace. More often than not, a positive corporate image is overstated. Nonetheless, take advantage of the publicity and positioning to grow in your markets. Lasting corporate images are built in a variety of ways. Learn a lesson from Steve Jobs, who manifested a special talent for using image to communicate his vision. Apple Computer molded its image based on superior products, an exciting work environment, and its self-proclaimed mission to change the world. Apple cared only about making the personal computer a way of life at work, at school, and in the home.

Build a Supporting Cast

After starting Apple Computer, Steve Jobs put on shoes, shaved his whiskers, and kept his hair fashionably long. Jobs preferred bow ties, suspenders, and designer jeans over three-piece business suits. This was a big change from his counterculture days when shoulder-length hair, a scraggly beard, and bare feet were part of the dress code.

Steve Jobs was founder, chairman of the board, and front man for Apple Computer. He recruited Mike Markkula, a retired 38-year-old millionaire as his CEO. Markkula then tapped Michael Scott, a former National Semiconductor executive, as Apple's president. These experienced businessmen added behind-the-scenes stability to the hypergrowth start-up.

Once Apple reached $1 billion in sales, Jobs went looking for a new CEO who could extend the company's hypergrowth. He lured John Sculley, the 44-year-old marketing whiz of the Pepsi-Cola Company with a $2 million bonus, an annual salary of $2 million, and options on 350,000 shares of Apple stock. Sculley brought to Apple his Fortune 500 credibility and the skills to establish a global presence.

Find Investors and Sponsors

Apple aligned itself with key investors and sponsors. Mike Markkula introduced Steve Jobs to several well-known financiers whose experience and reputations were worth far more than their investments. These early investors included Hank Smith, general partner of the Rockefeller family's venture capital firm; Arthur Rock, one of the best judges of high-tech start-ups; and Henry Singleton, chairman of Teledyne Inc. They not only put up money, these sponsors helped Apple anticipate pitfalls, minimize tax liabilities, and create new distribution channels.

Manage the Media

Apple was at its image best with the introduction of the Macintosh computer. First it created a $400,000 TV commercial based on the Orwellian novel *1984*. The 60-second spot depicted rows of uniformed ciphers with shaved heads staring at Big Brother droning on from a giant movie screen. Suddenly, a young athletic woman emerged from the ranks and hurled a sledgehammer through the screen, which vaporized in blinding white light. The commercial announced the introduction of the Macintosh computer. Although the spot aired only once during the Super Bowl, it was replayed hundreds of times by the media over the next several weeks.

Apple spent $15 million in advertising in the first 100 days of the Macintosh launch. Suppliers attended day-long training seminars. Journalists were sent plastic lunch boxes containing press information and Macintosh T-shirts. Steve Jobs and John Sculley conducted some 60 media interviews, which led to a dozen trade magazines featuring the Macintosh on their covers. Apple printed 10 million copies of a 20-page magazine insert. By the end of its campaign, Macintosh was positioned as the second desk appliance—after the telephone.

Get to the Market Makers

Early on, Apple retained the services of public relations guru, Regis McKenna. He planted stories about Apple throughout key trade and consumer publications. Apple also found its way onto the desk of Ben Rosen, the most influential electronics analyst on Wall Street. Rosen's use of an Apple computer was a great endorsement for the Silicon Valley start-up.

MANAGE YOUR RESEARCH

Most hypergrowth corporations depend on research to provide a clear definition of emerging opportunities in the marketplace. Once hypergrowth kicks in, research shows how to improve sales, reduce costs, and improve competitive positions. David Norman was a world-class researcher. He created Dataquest, Inc., to document the semiconductor, office equipment, electronics, computer, telecommunications, and construction machinery industries. After Dataquest was acquired by A.C. Nielsen Company, and Norman realized he'd never run the parent company, he started a computer retail chain called Businessland.

Isolate the Best Opportunities

Businessland's early research uncovered three big growth markets: white collar workers, home office workers, and replacement buyers. Since fewer than one-third of all white-collar workers used computers, Businessland could "cherry pick" until saturation reached two-thirds of the 62 million people in this market. While most home office workers required business-level computers, only 10 percent of them had one. Finally, the huge replacement market provided another growth opportunity for Businessland. This market consisted of computer users who needed to upgrade to state-of-the-art, or simply a better level of equipment.

Locate the Core Customers

The fact that 80 percent of Businessland's sales were to the nation's 1,000 largest companies resulted from detailed research. David Norman knew more about connecting PCs to mainframe computers than any of his competitors. He also knew who was planning to place volume PC orders to build their local area networks.

Get the Right Data

David Norman dismissed much of the industry research that predicted a buying slowdown. Norman refuted the reports because industry researchers focused mostly on small computer specialty stores. Norman knew that two-thirds of the personal computer business came from the business market—data not picked up by the researchers. When Norman did spot a buying slowdown among his Fortune 1,000 clients, he overlayed this data onto his business plan and made adjustments. Businessland refocused and tooled up with state-of-the-art PC technology, systems integration services, and trained personnel.

MANAGE YOUR EMPLOYEES

Managing employees in a hypergrowth environment requires innovation and flexibility. Employees need room to try new ideas without the risk of losing their jobs. Successful hypergrowth managers assess risks while encouraging innovation. Fred Smith provides a model of how to manage employees throughout hypergrowth.

Become a Hands-On Manager

Fred Smith's philosophy was simply to hire the best people, give them the best training, and provide them with the best possible compensation. In return, his employees provided top-notch service that translated into corporate profits.

Smith created a distinct corporate culture at Federal Express, congealed by his infectious form of enthusiasm. He rewards outstanding work with Bravo Zulu stickers, based on the Navy signal flags meaning "job well done."

Federal Express never unionized because Fred Smith promised to stay closely involved with his employees. As a result, Smith, James Barksdale, the chief operating officer and James Perkins, senior vice-president of personnel, devote every Tuesday morning to hearing complaints from employees who believed they were disciplined unfairly. Smith's hands-on management style reverses about 20 percent of the decisions. If the "hearings" are delayed, employees win by default.

Federal Express operates with a "share-the-wealth" philosophy through promotions from within, profit sharing, and no-furloughs. Fred Smith asserts that if he manages his employees well, then unions won't be needed.

Reward Productivity

Federal Express rewards productivity through its MBO/PBO program. This management-by-objective/project-by-objective program focuses more on results than on the methods used to achieve them. In the MBO/PBO program, managers and senior-level employees can earn cash bonuses on the basis of their accomplishments relative to the company's performance.

Smith also provides incentives to his 3,000 part-time employees (mostly college students) who work the midnight shift at the Superhub. If students maintain their grades during the day and win the package sorting battle at night, Federal Express pays 75 percent of their college tuition.

Another example of rewarding productivity is the Federal Express Modified Duty/Rehabilitation program. This innovative approach to disability saved Federal Express more than $4 million after just one year of operation. Employees who injure themselves typically receive 70 percent of their salary for up to 26 weeks on disability. Smith's Modified Rehab program gets disabled workers back on the job quickly since they earn between 71 percent and 100 percent of their pay under reassignment. Disabled workers perform other duties until they can return to their original positions. The program improved productivity, cut down on overtime, and eliminated the need for temporary help.

MANAGE YOUR MANAGERS

Managing managers is like conducting an orchestra. Your job is to coordinate their performances through shared values and a common goal. Hire and train managers who are more talented than you are in their particular areas. Provide these managers with structure, education, and training so they can adapt to change. You must train your managers to enhance the performance of those they manage. When this occurs, sales, service, market share, profitability, and quality will all improve.

Prepare a Trained Replacement

At Computer Associates, Charles Wang requires each manager to prepare a trained replacement. He likes to move his managers, without warning, into new challenges when the opportunities present themselves. Managers that fit this mold are known as self-starting doers who welcome a challenge. Wang shifts managerial positions every couple of years to prevent boredom and provide new horizons. He typically dismisses most managers and executives from acquired companies because they don't fit into his corporate culture.

Apply Zero-Based Thinking

Charles Wang takes his company through a reorganization every year based on what he calls zero-based thinking. His managers must justify all over again what they are doing. He forces them to take a fresh look at their jobs and understand why they work at Computer Associates. Wang trains his managers to keep an eye on the bottom line. His official management motto emphasizes this corporate value: "It is our most important month in our most important quarter."

MANAGE YOUR CUSTOMERS

To manage your customers, listen closely for what they need, yet don't receive. Your customers will either teach you something you didn't know or help you determine what they really want. Customers will also show you how to diversify your products and services, maximize your stated benefits, and improve your merchandising. Successful customer management requires that you stay close to your customers so you know how they live, work, and play.

Know the Customer

Liz Claiborne grew quickly because she discovered that she served two types of customers—consumers and retailers. Liz

Claiborne's first commandment was to "Satisfy Thy Consumer" and her second tenent was to "Support Thy Retailer." Zealous adherence to these guidelines sparked Liz Claiborne's hypergrowth.

Respond to Consumer Needs

Liz Claiborne satisfies her consumers because she responds to their needs with a constant flow of fresh merchandise. Her six fashion seasons mean that consumers can always find summer outfits in July. Ten Liz Claiborne fashion specialists visit stores, talk with customers, photograph displays, and give tips to salespeople. They spend all their time figuring out ways to better service consumers.

Support the Retailer

Liz Claiborne maintains an extensive support system for her network of retailers. Liz knows that if her clothing lines aren't effectively merchandised, all of her efforts in design and production are lost. Trained retail specialists visit hundreds of stores each year to present merchandising clinics for salespeople and department managers.

Store personnel learn how to display the Liz Claiborne collections. They also learn about Claiborne's history, goals, and fashion points of view. The most important thing they learn is that Liz Claiborne cares equally about the retailer and the consumer and expects store personnel to, in turn, care as much.

Claiborne's initial contact with retailers occurs at her New York showroom. Up to 65 salespeople work the showroom in lieu of a road salesforce. When retailers come to New York, Claiborne's top management team is available to meet their needs and support their goals.

MANAGE YOUR COMPETITORS

One of the best ways to manage your competitors is to provide the absolute best in products and services. Then, become the world's foremost in your field with an unquestioned reputation for integrity and quality. You'll soon find every competitor trying to emulate your success. Managing your competitors requires a revolutionary business spirit and a tough-minded, disciplined work ethic.

Take the Competition Seriously

Leslie Wexner takes his competitors very seriously since the valuation of The Limited's shares depends on its growth rate. At one point, in fact, more than a dozen institutional investors cut their Limited holdings because they couldn't see how Wexner could sustain his growth rate. Wexner figured that as sales expanded, competition held the key to growth. Wexner acquired vulnerable competitors, which increased the size and value of his company.

Go on the Offensive

Leslie Wexner never backs down from a competitor. He acquired Lane Bryant, Victoria's Secret, and Roaman's all in one year. Then he acquired Pic-A-Dilly, the Lerner chain, the prestigious Henri Bendel store, and the Abercrombie & Fitch units.

The Lane Bryant acquisition typifies Wexner's style. He eliminated the tallest and largest sizes because the volume didn't justify the inventory. He introduced sizes 14 through 20, since 40 percent of his customers fit this profile. Then Wexner changed the look of Lane Bryant by upgrading its styles. Just five years after he absorbed the Lane Bryant chain, its store count grew from 222 to 630 units.

Wexner then practically doubled the size of his operating base by acquiring Lerners. Considered the McDonald's of the clothing business, Wexner paid $297 million for the 770-store Lerner chain. Virtually bankrupt when he purchased it, Wexner discovered that Lerner's merchandise was out of step and overpriced. He turned the chain around by integrating its inventory into The Limited's distribution system and updating its fashion lines.

When Leslie Wexner invited Roy Raymond, the founder of Victoria's Secret, to Columbus, Ohio, they discussed the lingerie business and why Victoria's Secret wasn't more profitable. Wexner figured Raymond's five stores and periodic catalog could be expanded within The Limited's distribution system. Wexner envisioned a Victoria's Secret next to every Limited store since their customers were one and the same. Yet he contemplated for three years how to integrate Victoria's Secret into the Limited family of stores. Then he approached Raymond again with an offer to acquire the small chain. After Wexner purchased Victoria's Secret, he transformed it into America's fastest growing specialty retail enterprise.

Don't Let Size Hold You Back

Leslie Wexner attempted to acquire a company twice his size with an unsolicited offer to take over Carter Hawley Hale (CHH). However, CHH's primary lender, Bank of America, revised its loan agreements to state that all loans would default if control of the retailer changed hands. This dampened Wexner's enthusiasm because his lenders were wary of stepping into a default threat, no matter how artificial. So Wexner backed off.

Two years later, Wexner attempted to buy Carter Hawley Hale in an all-cash offer of $55 a share for stock trading at $35. To avert a takeover, CHH split into a specialty and a department store operation. When General Cinema Corp. obtained 50.1 percent voting interest in the specialty store spinoff, Wexner withdrew his $1.93 billion bid. Even in set-backs, such boldness typifies Wexner's tough-minded and revolutionary spirit.

MANAGE YOUR NETWORK

Before hypergrowth kicks in, form a network of players who can influence the market's attitude and buying decisions. Use in-house newsletters to provide detailed information about your products and services; electronic bulletin boards to stay in close contact with suppliers; broadcast fax machines to send out hundreds of press releases to the media; videotapes and conference calls to control message content. For nationwide gatherings, consider closed-circuit television to downlink broadcasts at hotels.

Get Plugged In

Compaq Chairman, Ben Rosen, was particularly well-connected in the personal computer industry. His electronic rolodex kept track of 2,700 computer executives, vendors, distributors, media, and end-user customers. Rosen knew the value of personal relationships since Compaq's technology was sold primarily by word-of-mouth. Rosen cultivated his contacts as he frequently sent them "insider" information about Compaq and its products.

Overcome the F.U.D. Factor

Compaq once rallied its network to overcome the F.U.D. (Fear/Uncertainty/Doubt) Factor. To build market momentum at the unveiling of its Deskpro 386, Rod Canion shared the stage with Bill Gates, Microsoft's Chairman, and Gordon Moore, Intel's Chairman. These superstars, together with heads of a dozen other software companies, testified to Deskpro's compatibility with existing industry standards. This impressive gathering added credibility to Compaq's new product launch and eliminated the F.U.D. Factor.

MANAGE YOUR COSTS

One way to achieve hypergrowth is to provide better products for more people at lower costs. Companies that establish product manufacturing outside the United States can take advantage of lower labor costs when it comes time to expand production capacity. Running a lean operation teaches you how to compete when production volumes drop or when your market becomes saturated.

Reduce Production Costs

Seagate Technology became the industry's low-cost disk drive manufacturer when it established plants in Singapore and Bangkok. Alan Shugart trained more than 100 foreign workers at Seagate's California headquarters. They learned their lessons well as Seagate soon outproduced its Japanese competitors to become the world's low-cost disk drive manufacturer.

Seagate realized early on that disk drives would someday be subject to commodity pricing. So they invest millions of dollars each year into materials research to lower production expense, lower material costs, and achieve better yields.

Increase Production Capacity

Seagate jumped first into the 5¹/₄-inch disk drive business. Soon it boosted production capacity to 50,000 units a day, up from 12,000 units two years earlier. This added capacity gave Seagate the ability to produce huge volumes and pass on the cost savings. When Seagate shifted into production of its 3¹/₂-inch disk drives, it invested nearly $100 million to add 32,000 square feet of production space in Singapore and transform its Thailand facility to assemble and test the new disk drives.

Dump Surplus Inventory

Seagate's hard disk drives cut the cost of storing data by 95 percent as its manufacturing capacity expanded to more than 2 million disk drives per quarter. Unfortunately for Seagate, the market demand peaked at 1.3 million drives per quarter. After Apple canceled an order for 100,000 disk drives, Seagate's inventories reached record-high levels. In order to deplete its $300 million inventory, Seagate reduced prices by 25 percent. Price slashing also drove marginal competitors out of the business.

MANAGE YOUR CASH FLOW

Cash flow represents a company's earnings after depreciation and before taxes. As a standard barometer of success, cash flow is a critical hypergrowth dynamic. TCI, for instance, fueled hypergrowth with its $1 billion cash flow. Secure in its market position and confident of its cash flow strength, TCI shunned shareholder earnings and focused instead on maximizing shareholder value.

Maximize Cash Flow

TCI's $1 billion cash flow exceeded that of Time Inc. and surpassed the Big Three TV networks combined. During its hypergrowth, TCI used every means available to maximize cash flow. It accelerated depreciation deductions, took investment tax credits, and retained full deductions by avoiding limited partnerships. TCI's cash flow gave it an edge in its mergers-and-acquisitions activities. John Malone never feared taking on new debt when acquiring cable franchises because he deducted the interest payments, added value to his company, and increased TCI's cash flow with new subscribers.

Build Equity

With its phenomenal cash flow, TCI's $4.6 billion debt appeared less imposing. In light of its liquidity, TCI's earnings averaged less than a quarter a share for its hypergrowth decade. Perfectly content to report low earnings and take on debt, TCI preserved cash flow by not paying out dividends. John Malone preferred, instead, to build equity. Since he was not concerned with investor opinions or quarterly earnings, Malone bid aggressively for asset-building, cash flow-generating, cable subscribers.

MANAGE YOUR MARGINS

Operating margins represent the difference between a product's cost and its profit before interest and income taxes. Increasing margins is accomplished either by raising prices, lowering costs, or both. Despite cost pressures caused by a weakening dollar, higher material costs, and rising manufacturing costs, Reebok's operating profit margins remained steady at 30 percent during its hypergrowth decade.

Control Pricing Factors

Reebok's tight control over selling prices fueled its hypergrowth. However, premium pricing was not the only reason for Reebok's steady margin performance. Low levels of close-out merchandise, limited channels of distribution, fast inventory turns, and controlled overhead expenses helped Reebok successfully manage its margins.

Lower Operating Expenses

Paul Fireman also lowered operating expenses to keep Reebok's edge. Since Reebok didn't own manufacturing plants, it avoided fixed-cost coverages. Reebok also reduced variable costs, such as Pentland Industries' inspection, shipping, and administration fees. Its financing costs declined as a result of reduced borrowing. Then, with proceeds from its common stock sales, Reebok decreased interest expense on bank loans and interest-bearing accounts payable. Due to its economies of scale, Reebok also decreased its general and administrative expenses. Finally, Paul Fireman reduced costs more by lowering Reebok's sales commission structure.

MANAGE YOUR ASSETS

Hypergrowth occurs when capital and labor can solve emerging problems more efficiently than the competition. Build a strong management team that can establish and manage an asset base. The Price Club's asset management skills are reflected in its volume output per worker, which averages $500,000 per year per full-time employee.

Build Corporate Assets

The Price Club built a large cash reserve by issuing $200 million of debentures at a 5.5 percent interest rate. The debentures, convertible into corporate stock at $51.00 per share, became the means for The Price Club to build its huge asset base. When the dust cleared, Robert Price had accumulated a $250 million cash reserve. With no bank debt and essentially no mortgage debt, The Price Club used its war chest to fuel rapid expansion into new markets.

Control the Assets

Robert Price put his cash reserves to work when he opened new warehouses and purchased surplus properties around those stores. As land values increased, surplus properties were sold at a handsome profit. The Price Club's nonwarehouse properties also generated rental income.

Real estate ownership served as a strategic source of value for stockholders. It helped The Price Club reduce occupancy costs and avoid lease negotiations tied to sales. The company's 42 owned facilities offer 10 million square feet of warehouse operating space.

Preserve Those Assets

The Price Club preserved its assets through operational efficiencies. For example, rather than expand product assortment to attact more retail customers, The Price Club actually limited inventory to keep out the casual shopper. They concentrated on small groups of dedicated retail customers and holders of business licenses. Its membership fee promotes the idea that shopping at The Price Club is a privilege not accorded everyone.

Other operational efficiencies enhanced The Price Club's assets. They leveraged vendors' accounts payable since inventories turned faster than the allowed time to pay for them. Finally, The Price Club didn't pay a cash dividend since it would be taxed once as corporate income and again as personal income to its shareholders.

MANAGE YOUR TECHNOLOGY

One of the benefits of well-managed technology is how it can improve productivity. For example, a meeting conducted from your headquarters can be viewed in hundreds of store locations nationwide. Live discussions of your goals and strategies can be shared with all employees. Price rollbacks can be simultaneously implemented. Computer sales figures can be instantly updated and reviewed with all managers. The impact of new policies can be discussed as they unfold. Sound too good to be true? This is exactly how Sam Walton manages Wal-Mart technology to stay close to his 275,000 associates.

Make the Technology Commitment

Five years before hypergrowth began, Wal-Mart installed computer terminals in every store. Its state-of-the-art network was designed to do everything from track inventory to pick expansion sites.

Wal-Mart then launched the world's largest private satellite network. It provided two-way voice and data exchange and one-way video transmission. Wal-Mart can now beam information back and forth between its Bentonville, Arkansas, headquarters and more than 1,200 stores. This network took nearly three years to design and cost more than $20 million to launch.

Reduce Operating Costs

Sam Walton's commitment to information technology reduced Wal-Mart's operating costs to just 20 percent of sales, the lowest for any discounter or major retailer. Advanced technology reduced Wal-Mart's telephone, payroll, and occupancy costs while increasing its inventory turnover.

On the store receiving front, Wal-Mart's Universal Price Code system saved about 60 percent of the man-hours previously required to process deliveries. Stocking crews read UPC bar codes from container labels using hand-held laser scanners. Wal-Mart's computerized distribution equipment investment totaled just 1.7 percent of sales—again, lowest in the discount industry.

Improve Productivity

Wal-Mart gained big dividends from its technology investments: Improved data communications, faster check-out service, more accurate credit card authorizations, and fewer delays. High-speed communications technology replaced 400 rural telephone companies, many which didn't even offer Touch Tone telephone service. Sophisticated technology improved communication among stores, enhancing distribution, and boosting sales.

MANAGE YOUR SUPPLIERS

Train your suppliers to understand that the only reason for their existence is to help increase your sales. Suppliers respond to your hypergrowth needs when you teach them, then beat on them, to stay focused. For example, the 18-man Home Depot merchandising staff is responsible for purchasing 25,000 different stock keeping units for each of its 118 stores from 3,000 different suppliers. Merchandisers stay on top of vendors as each store's total inventory turns over every eight weeks.

Train Yourself First

Home Depot management first trained itself, then trained its suppliers. During start-up, Home Depot founders played an active role in training vendors. Bernard Marcus was the store's furniture buyer, Arthur Blank was the electrical buyer, and Pat Farrah ordered everything else. As they beat deals out of vendors, Home Depot favored those suppliers who understood their business and supported their goals.

Vendors learned early on that Home Depot's initial buying decisions were made at the corporate level by merchandise managers. Reorders were then placed by store management personnel. Home Depot also purchased from overseas suppliers whose products were sold by the company under private brand-name labels.

Demand Concessions from Vendors

Home Depot merchandisers are involved in everything from store set-up to vendor relations. They are trained to demand concessions from vendors, including favorable shipping dates. Home Depot gets an automatic 5 percent discount if it has to maintain inventory for a vendor under contract. Merchandisers push vendors to help train in-store salespeople to sell their products. They even strong-arm vendors to affix bar codes on plywood and dowels to speed up check out lines.

Store managers are trained to sell as much product as they can while merchandisers ride vendors to keep the shelves stocked. Home Depot's merchandisers depend on the Suggested Order Quantity (SOQ) system to guide vendors toward effective inventory management.

Water Their Camels

In exchange for top service, Home Depot provides vendors with great name recognition and fast turnover. Many manufacturers credit Home Depot for helping them become more effective competitors. Home Depot offers vendors new retailing opportunities such as adding coupons to packages and providing in-store advertising.

MANAGE YOUR BUREAUCRATS

Government and politics is a business discipline just like marketing, finance, and engineering. Hypergrowth requires that you learn how to deal effectively with bureaucrats including lawyers, judges, politicians, regulators, and others involved in the government process. Learn to manage your bureaucrats because government plays a major role in how you conduct business. Through years of antitrust litigation, Bill McGowan and MCI became experts at handling their bureaucrats.

Educate Callow Advocates

When dealing with bureaucrats, McGowan realized that they were bright young people who lacked business experience. They often did not understand MCI, its markets, or the economic implications of their actions. So McGowan made it his business to educate them. If they were lawyers, he brought in lawyers to talk with them. If they were economists, he drew them economic models.

Play to Win

Bill McGowan became an expert at explaining the realities of his situation to bureaucrats—but in their language. He made it plain that if they did something wrong, he wouldn't hesitate to appeal it. As a result, MCI spent years in appellate court. Its victories increased credibility with the same bureaucrats in subsequent meetings.

MANAGE YOUR MANUFACTURERS

Hypergrowth requires global manufacturing sources to keep production costs low. When going global, you need a set of guidelines to help you manage your foreign manufacturers. First, increase the number of contract manufacturers. This will expand your production capacity and provide a diversity of sources. Next, be sure to specify your quality control standards and reject products that don't meet these specs. Finally, arrange for inspection of finished goods prior to shipment. Then enforce financial penalties for shipments that don't meet your standards.

Require Zero Defects

Compaq's reputation for demanding zero defects is so prevalent that it requires zero-defect programs for everyone of its suppliers. Zero defects helped Compaq increase its operating pace. While computer manufacturers can take anywhere from 12 months to 4 years to develop and introduce new products, Compaq averages 9 months, which includes construction of new factories.

Demand Peak Performance

Compaq's success lies in its ability to improve upon the personal computer standard. Its fast-paced performance is complimented by innovations such as dual-made monitors, internal fixed disk drives, the highest degree of compatibility in the industry, and of course, zero defects. Compaq demands peak performance from each of its suppliers. It will return an entire shipment of components if just one defect is discovered.

Keep a Fluid Structure

Compaq's tight reign on manufacturing resulted in lower inventory levels and increased gross margins. Chips are made in the same building where executives work. This arrangement gives Compaq total inventory control and quick turnaround. Compaq's principal manufacturing facility is located on 150 acres in Houston, Texas, along with manufacturing sites in Singapore and Scotland.

Compaq manages its product cycle by introducing more powerful machines just as the market starts to taper. At one point, Compaq's manufacturing team put out so many new products that Rod Canion restructured his organization into four functional groups: marketing, engineering, sales, and manufacturing. He then centralized marketing to make sure its new models did not cannibalize sales of Compaq's current offerings.

TRAITS OF SUCCESSFUL HYPERGROWTH MANAGEMENT

You set the tone for your company through your attitude and actions. Believe it or not, hypergrowth CEOs are ordinary people who have simply managed to achieve extraordinary results in the marketplace. Although they share many traits in common, above all these CEOs are resourceful, generous, prudent, bold, and resiliant:

Trait 1: Resourceful

- Leslie Wexner promotes from within so The Limited managers become vice presidents of distribution and clerks become merchandising managers.
- Selig Zises gathered recognized experts from diverse fields to design innovative investment products for Integrated Resources and its investors.
- Sam Walton designed Wal-Mart's educational programs, which include The Walton Institute of Retailing, Retail Management Training Services, Sam's Operating School, and The Department Managers' Development Guide. These workshops and seminars help each associate maximize their service to customers.

Trait 2: Generous

- Rod Canion designed Compaq's management system to include unlimited sick leave, stock options for all permanent employees, and all the free soda employees can consume.
- Charles Wang doesn't count pennies when it comes to employee welfare—Computer Associates spends millions of dollars a year for daily breakfasts as trucks deliver muffins,

doughnuts, fresh fruit, and beverages to its 6,500 employees worldwide.

- John Malone keeps managers and top executives happy through special perks. TCI management, for example, acquired 21 percent of Liberty Tele-Communications in exchange for cable television properties valued at $4 million. Six years after TCI exchanged Liberty stock for TCI shares, the value of management's original investment had increased ten-fold.

Trait 3: Prudent

- Robert Price, The Price Club CEO, ranked first among all American executives for profits relative to a CEO's pay three years in a row.

- Fred Smith maintains, at most, five management layers between himself and any nonmanagement Federal Express employee in his company which has more than 50,000 people on payroll.

- To grow quickly and insulate the Home Depot against competition, Bernard Marcus created a manager's bonus program that compensates managers according to sales, return on assets (ROA), and gross margin return on investment (GMROI). This program rewards productivity, increases operating income, promotes slow-moving inventory for quick sales, and frees up much needed shelf space.

Trait 4: Bold

- Paul Fireman attracts dynamic, bright, and highly motivated individuals to Reebok. Not bound by tradition or unions, he often hires people with little experience in the shoe industry, but with skills in managing a billion-dollar company.

- As its divisions multiplied, Liz Claiborne brought on quality managers to keep the operation running smoothly. Liz gave up her passion for design to edit the work of others and train new design talent.

- Bill McGowan runs MCI with a hands-off management style. He has a steady goal and leaves the details to others.

Trait 5: Resiliant

- David Norman transitioned from a fighter pilot to a researcher to a technician to a salesman to a manager as he built Businessland into a billion-dollar global enterprise.
- Alan Shugart took Seagate from start-up to hypergrowth, then into constriction as his products were rendered obsolete by new technology. Subsequently, product breakthroughs in growth segments put Shugart back on the hypergrowth fast track.
- After starting Apple Computer and taking it through the billion-dollar barrier in record time, Steve Jobs was forced out of his own company. Jobs simply started another computer company that is destined for hypergrowth.

Since billion-dollar companies are not built in a vacuum, you'll need to hone your management skills to communicate your dynamic vision. Then you'll want to raise up smart teams to develop organizational modus operandi capable of creating and sustaining hypergrowth. You can do it!

7

Get It There Fast!

Distribution is how products get from manufacturer to consumer as distributors link producers with end-users. Like most systems, over the years, distribution has been redesigned and improved. Hypergrowth requires a flexible distribution infrastructure for quick response to early signs of market change. Successful distributors depend on speed, innovation, discipline, and a clear vision of the future to differentiate themselves from the competition.

While the delivery of goods is its primary purpose, distribution now offers an extensive array of support services. Financial and logistical support help reduce costs, increase productivity, streamline operations, and consolidate information. Hypergrowth is dependent upon distribution effectiveness: If you can't deliver the goods once you create the demand, you're out of business.

Channels of distribution can provide immediate access to specific markets for any type of product. They also fulfill other important functions such as warehousing and transporting of products, communicating customer needs, assisting with marketing services, and providing credit to buyers. Choosing a distribution channel is an important corporate decision. Once a top-quality channel is in place, new products become easy to introduce. A well-established distributor can also serve as an

143

entry barrier for competitors. All these factors are crucial to hypergrowth success.

HOW TO ACHIEVE HYPERGROWTH DISTRIBUTION

For hypergrowth distribution to occur you need to:

- *Know Your Market.* Juxtapose your market's changing needs against the strengths and weaknesses of all current and potential competitors. Commit to service only those markets that align with your company's strengths.
- *Collapse the Time Float.* Rapid delivery reduces costs, improves efficiency, and eliminates delays. Trained employees responding to customer needs can eliminate the lag between order and delivery.
- *Extract Quality Information.* Accurate and timely information is a strategic asset when it provides a competitive advantage. Critical distribution information focuses on changes in market size, product use, competitive positions, customer behavior, and operating margins.
- *Integrate New Technologies.* It is not enough for computers to track the flow of goods. Hypergrowth requires state-of-the-art distribution applications to provide an edge over the competition.
- *Improve Productivity.* Distribution leadership requires optimum use of corporate resources such as personnel, technology, and capital. Distribution productivity can offset declines in gross margins when competitive pricing occurs.
- *Provide Value-Added Services.* Value-added distribution bonds the relationship between supplier and customer. Competitors often find such channels difficult to penetrate and duplicate.
- *Find New Partners.* Hypergrowth requires resources and skills rarely found in one company. Partnering in the

distribution channel can provide access to new opportunities created by a rapidly changing market.

Know Your Options

Distributors come in all sizes. Small ones offer the benefits of close ties to customers and suppliers, owner involvement, flexibility, and quick delivery. Larger distributors provide economies of scale, national contracts, inventory resources, buying power, strong support services, and diversified product groups. Several variations of traditional distribution models have sparked the hypergrowth phenomenon.

WHOLESALE DISTRIBUTION

Wholesale distribution involves a wide range of intermediaries including the direct salesforce, manufacturers' representatives, and distributors. Reebok distributes its athletic footwear through a small nationwide sales staff. They also contract with independent commercial sales reps who exclusively handle the Reebok line. Since consumers often judge shoe brand quality by distribution quality, Reebok picks only the best merchandisers to carry its products. Its 5,000 nationwide distributors include pro shops, athletic specialty stores, sporting goods stores, and upscale department stores.

Image and margins are a top priority in Reebok's distribution strategy. Paul Fireman knows that for shoe demand to stay high, he cannot distribute through every store. Because image is determined by where a shoe is sold, Reebok avoids discount retailers.

Pentland Industries plc, a British shoe intermediary, manages Reebok's shoe distribution from overseas manufacturing sites. They inspect the finished goods, facilitate shipment from foreign ports, and arrange for payment to manufacturers.

Late deliveries and scheduling problems plagued Reebok's hypergrowth. At one point, shoes arrived months late for the back-to-school season. Reebok decided to work closer with retailers to develop acceptable order and delivery schedules. Focusing on retailer needs was a key factor in Reebok's success. Retailers responded by providing the prime selling space and promotional support that sustained consumer interest and fueled Reebok's hypergrowth.

Wholesale Distribution Channels

Successful wholesale distribution requires both a broad product assortment and a rapid response to the needs of local retailers. Wholesale intermediaries include the direct salesforce, manufacturers' representatives, and distributors.

- *Direct salesforce* markets products from the company's headquarters, sales branches, and field offices. They call on wholesale distributors, who in turn call on dealers and end-user customers. Since a direct salesforce devotes its time to selling one company's product line, they keep close customer contact. This permits firsthand study of market needs, which leads to long-term customer loyalty. Selling direct provides customers with better service, volume discounts, and detailed product information.
- *Manufacturer's representatives* (reps) substitute for a direct salesforce. Agents sell related product lines in exclusive territories. They don't take title to the goods because manufacturers ship and bill purchasers directly. The manufacturer's representative is just one type of agent middleman. Others include brokers, commission merchants, resident buyers, and sales agents. Reps allow manufacturers to concentrate on product-line expansion without the expense of establishing sales offices. They can also field test new products and report early results back to the manufacturer.
- *Distributors* are a ready-made salesforce. They provide manufacturers with quick product entry, knowledge of local market needs, and access to buyers. Straight commission distributors let companies predetermine their selling expense, eliminate personnel recruiting, and minimize

training costs. They also reduce credit problems and storage costs. However, feedback regarding market acceptance, final product conditions, local advertising response, and inquiry follow-up is often limited.

PULL-THROUGH DISTRIBUTION

Pull-through distribution at Wal-Mart starts with a giant warehouse surrounded by 175 stores over a 200-square-mile area. A typical 650,000-square-foot Wal-Mart warehouse services its stores within a six-hour driving radius to insure daily product deliveries. Wal-Mart's 10 distribution facilities process about 80 percent of its goods sold.

These company-owned-and-operated distribution centers function on a pull-premise. Individual Wal-Mart stores tell the distribution centers where, when, and how much merchandise is needed. The distribution centers then fulfill the orders, helping Wal-Mart to achieve market saturation, which fuels its hypergrowth.

Wal-Mart's pull-through distribution model is technology-dependent. Its mainframe computers network with each store's minicomputer. Wal-Mart also launched the world's largest private satellite system to transmit voice, data, and video around-the-clock between its Arkansas headquarters and more than 1,200 locations. Finally, its revolutionary point-of-sale scanning of universal price code-marked goods was adapted to sort shipments at its distribution centers.

Pull-through distribution requires instant information to monitor and fulfill customer needs. Wal-Mart's sophisticated communications system improves service and product selection. It provides rapid credit card authorizations, analyzes computerized sales information hourly, and transmits training videos to all store locations.

Pull-Through Distribution Technologies

Effective pull-through distribution integrates state-of-the-art technology to improve productivity, reduce costs, provide value-added services, and enhance management decision making. The technologies include:

- *Mainframe computers* are still at the heart of a distribution information network. While small and medium-sized companies have shifted toward centralized mainframe environments, larger distributors have established decentralized information systems with dedicated computers at each location.

- *Personal computers* have put computing power into the hands of managers. The PC distribution applications include inventory management, fixed asset control, order entry, cash management, shipment routing, personnel productivity measurements, bid analysis, facilities management, direct marketing, list maintenance, strategic modeling, online database searches, vehicle management, and catalog design.

- *Telecommunications* combines telephones, computers, satellites, fiber optics, videophones, teleconferencing, voice mailboxes, videocassetes, videodisks, computer-based mail systems, videotext, and mobile communications. It is the vital link between customers and suppliers in the distribution channel. Telecommunications created warehousing and distribution productivity breakthroughs with online inventory availability checking.

- *Bar code scanning* transformed distribution through order picking, invoice pricing, order billing, merchandise tracking, inventory control, receiving, shipping, merchandise ticketing, security, employee tracking, merchandise inspection, returned goods processing, inventory control, employee identification, cash receipts recording, and catalog ordering.

- *Software* applications in distribution include transaction systems, online accounting, sales analysis, online order entry, inventory control systems, customer analysis, product profitability analysis, management decision support, automatic purchase order, delivery route scheduling, scanning, shelf layout, and interactive training.

MANUFACTURER-DIRECT DISTRIBUTION

Home Depot purchases its merchandise from more than 1,200 manufacturers who then ship the products directly to each store. This manufacturer-direct distribution strategy eliminated costly intermediaries and the added expense of central warehousing.

Since Home Depot purchases directly from manufacturers in huge quantities, it negotiates the lowest available prices. Home Depot merchandisers order directly through distribution centers to bypass vendor field service reps. This often creates confusion with vendor salesforces. However, manufacturers have responded to Home Depot merchandisers by providing additional purchasing and distribution conveniences.

For example, merchandisers at Home Depot demanded that suppliers adapt to its distribution strategy. They negotiated for better terms and service, particularly when it involved shipping dates, volume discounts, payment schedules, advertising allowances, and merchandising assistance. Home Depot even pushed manufacturers to provide better information on its packages to make their products easier to sell.

Home Depot carries a surplus of inventory at its stores to avoid stockouts. Its broad selections are warehoused right on the sales floor. This tactic increases customer convenience, minimizes out-of-stock occurrences, and lowers handling costs.

Types of Manufacturer-Direct Distributor

Most companies don't have the resources or skills to buy directly from manufacturers. Therefore, they take advantage of services and ordering conveniences from among four types of distributors. Each is distinguished by the amount of service provided, range of functions performed, and the extent of product-lines carried:

- *Full-line distributors* often stock up to 10,000 industrial items, reach wide horizontal markets, and provide one-stop ordering.

- *Specialized distributors* concentrate on products requiring a high degree of information or technical support.

- *Limited-line distributors* tend to be small and specialize in a dozen or so unrelated product-lines that require fast delivery and on-site stocking.

- *Departmentalized distributors* carry a full line of products that are grouped into departments for the sake of better merchandise management.

HUB-AND-SPOKE DISTRIBUTION

Federal Express pioneered the concept of centralized distribution for express package delivery. Known as hub-and-spoke distribution, logistics for this unique routing system utilized airports for the hubs and truck routes as its spokes.

Packages requiring next-day delivery are gathered, loaded onto planes, then flown to the Superhub in Memphis. Every night between midnight and 2:00 A.M., 3,000 employees and 60 aircraft gather at the Superhub's 1.5-million-square-foot complex to sort express packages. The 44-mile conveyor belt system, centralizes all parcels, divides them into 17 broad groups based on location, then resorts them into 600 geographic groups. The jets are reloaded and the packages forwarded on to their destinations.

Even though the system could sort 10,000 packages per hour on its opening night, Federal Express made just six overnight deliveries within an eleven-city network. However, in just over a decade, Federal Express exceeded its distribution sorting capacity of 1.2 million packages per night. To handle its growing volumes, Federal Express opened regional sorting centers in Newark, New Jersey, and Oakland, California. More than 30 percent of all deliveries soon bypassed the Superhub to capitalize on the cost difference between flying (60 cents/lb) and driving (12 cents/lb).

Federal Express Corporation's hub-and-spoke distribution system made the air express industry a vibrant part of the U.S.

transportation infrastructure. Its express delivery became a crucial link to the success of new business concepts such as "just-in-time" manufacturing.

Hub-and-Spoke Variations

The variations of hub-and-spoke distribution all attempt to eliminate redundant costs while providing value-added services. For companies that consider speed a vital asset, overnight delivery also reduces inventory carrying costs. Hub-and-spoke distribution provides a close working relationship among distributor, supplier, and customer. Its variations include:

- *Centralized warehousing* with stockless satellite distribution points that receive shipments from the major warehouse for local deliveries.
- *Full-line central warehousing* with subsidiary warehouses that stock only the fastest turning and most critical items.
- *Central offices* using telemarketing systems that serve regional distribution centers.

INTEGRATED DISTRIBUTION

The Limited operates an integrated distribution system to support its huge retail operation. Virtually all merchandise for Leslie Wexner's 3,095 stores gets shipped to the Columbus, Ohio, distribution facility where it is received, inspected, and marked with retail prices. This national distribution facility measures 2.6 million square feet—the size of 70 football fields. It processes more than 200 million pieces of merchandise each year.

Wexner's integrated distribution system maintains sufficient quantities of inventory to give his retail customers a full selection of the most current merchandise. The Limited's system can also stop shipment of any item and replace it with a fresh shipment within hours. Such adaptability helps The

Limited introduce new product lines as soon as they become available.

Using 747 jumbo jets, fashions are flown directly to the distribution center from thousands of American and foreign suppliers. Average processing time from arrival at the distribution center to shipment on to stores is two days with 99.9 percent accuracy. The Limited's procurement process resupplies hot items within weeks, compared to months for competitors. This integrated distribution system also generates top margins as merchandise is manufactured and distributed without the traditional middleman costs.

The Limited made a strategic distribution breakthrough when it acquired Mast Industries to coordinate all merchandise manufactured through off-shore suppliers. Mast worked with fewer, but larger, vendors to compress The Limited's already short ordering cycles.

Dynamics of Integrated Distribution

Integrated distribution can service hundreds of geographically disperse retail sites. Its effectiveness depends on market penetration, product selection, and support services. The functions of integrated distribution include:

- *Research* of customer needs and buying habits
- *Manufacturing* based on fashion styles, sizes, and materials
- *Promotions* including advertising and special sales events
- *Services* like delivery, credit, and in-home purchases
- *Testing* of new product ideas, positioning, and deletions
- *Pricing* levels like intermediate, sale, and final prices
- *Logistics* including transporting and warehousing.

EXCLUSIVE DISTRIBUTION

Compaq Computer pioneered the exclusive distribution channel through its authorized dealer network. From the start, its products have been offered to end users only through independent, full-service computer specialty dealers worldwide.

Compaq developed a loyal exclusive dealer network because it never sold computers directly to large corporations or through value-added resellers (VARs). VAR sales get channeled to dealers through its "Dealer Associate Program." Corporate customers, used to buying from a direct salesforce, found many of Compaq's authorized dealers providing field sales representatives to meet their needs.

Compaq designed computers that were 100 percent IBM-compatible. This meant no extra software or add-ons to clutter a dealer's inventory. Its noncompete sales posture also earned Compaq preferred shelf location within its exclusive distribution channel. Compaq's Salespaq Support Program provided authorized dealers with a wide variety of advertising, merchandising, service, and training incentives. Compaq also arranged for third-party financing to assist authorized dealers in extending payment terms on its products. Dealers provide pre-sale and post-sale support, training, installation, warranty, and post-warranty repair service.

Compaq's exclusive channel of distribution buffered its retailers during price wars. Since Compaq has no outside salesforce, it provides better margins than IBM and the clones. Since dealers receive the highest margins selling Compaq computers, they prefer to sell Compaq's products, especially when discounting occurs.

Exclusive Distribution Channel Parameters

Under an exclusive distribution arrangement, wholesale and retail sales are strictly limited by product line and geography. Often, only a single retailer is retained within a specific purchase region. An exclusive distribution channel can be established through the following steps:

- Calculate each market segment's sales potential.
- Determine which channels your competitors use and why.
- List the distribution requirements of your end users.

- Match the capabilities, costs, and resources of each distribution channel against the requirements dictated by your customers.

- Rank channels based on profit potential and ability to fulfill on requirements.

- Select and distribute exclusively through the channel offering the best balance of service and return on investment.

SELECTIVE DISTRIBUTION

Selective distribution is how Liz Claiborne maintains its designer looks without the designer price. Claiborne doesn't try to achieve widespread market coverage or high volume sales. Instead, she chooses selective distributors who deliver the prestige and margins of her clothing lines.

Liz Claiborne does not employ outside sales representatives or operate regional offices. Instead, sales and distribution are arranged through its New York City showroom. This helps management stay close to major customers. Virtually all of Claiborne's sales are made to 3,500 customer accounts in the United States that operate nearly 10,000 department and specialty stores. Yet, Claiborne's 100 largest customers generate 75 percent of the company's total sales volume.

Clothing manufactured domestically and overseas is first shipped to Claiborne's 500,000-square-foot distribution center in North Bergen, New Jersey. The outfits are then coordinated, reinspected, placed into modules, and shipped on to selective retailers.

Through its selective distribution channel, Liz Claiborne packaged its "store-within-a-store" concept. These consist of fully coordinated Claiborne accessories and apparel collections displayed over 7,000 square feet of department store space. Requiring a staff of trained fashion consultants, the displays are planned jointly by Claiborne's staff and store management.

Keys to Selective Distribution Success

The selective distribution strategy combines distribution channel control and prestige retailing. To achieve hypergrowth sales volumes, selective distribution requires:

- *Distributors* that are well-established, reputable stores
- *Customers* who are brand conscious and willing to travel a distance to purchase what they want
- *Marketing* that creates pleasant shopping conditions and excellent service.

RETAIL DISTRIBUTION

Integrated Resources established a nationwide retail distribution network comprised of 4,100 independent financial planners, hundreds of unaffiliated securities firms, and thousands of independent insurance agents.

Its financial planners are registered with its broker/dealer subsidiary, Integrated Resources Equity Corp. Since its financial planners pay their own marketing expenses, Integrated compensates them at a commission rate up to 90 percent of the premium payment. This is significantly higher than the securities industry's standard of 40 percent.

Integrated Resources formed The Integrated Resources Investment Centers to assist banks in distributing retail investment products. This retail distribution subsidiary offered mutual funds, annuities, and public limited partnerships to consumers holding nearly $2 trillion in savings products. These investment centers were made available only to commercial banks and thrifts with more than $500 million in assets. Since a 100 percent commission was paid on its product sales, this retail distribution strategy was actually a loss-leader for other Integrated Resources products.

Integrated Resources introduces new services in anticipation of new opportunities, closing down others when markets evaporate. For example, it created an international subsidiary to distribute Integrated Resources products in Europe and the Far East. It also discontinued operations of its energy division when oil and gas prices deteriorated.

Contents of a Retail Distribution Agreement

While a basic distributor's contract focuses on price, policy, territories, and responsibilities, a more detailed distribution agreement might include:

- Relationship between company and distribution channel
- The geography, industries, and customer types targeted
- Each party's marketing and service responsibilities
- Whether or not exclusive rights are granted
- Specific products sold and services rendered
- Full scope of services provided, including merchandising aids, product samples, education and training, sales call planning, and communication of market information
- A policy statement to cover conflicts such as crediting sales of national accounts within a middleman's territory or the handling of competing lines
- Projected annual sales volume three years out
- How costs, commissions, and bonuses are paid
- A list of customer benefits
- Policies for prices, terms, discounts, credit, invoices, collections, cancellations, changes, returns, and profit margins
- Who fulfills product warranties and guarantees
- Special rights held by each party
- Duration of the agreement and how it can be terminated.

WAREHOUSE DISTRIBUTION

The Price Club is not just retailing or wholesaling. It is actually a new form of distribution. As a discount retailer that benefited from the flaws in the wholesale distribution system, The Price Club based its success as much on logistics as on merchandising. Its average inventory turnover occurs every 16 days compared to every 90 days at discount stores or twice a year at full service retailers.

The Price Club operates without central warehousing as merchandise gets shipped directly to each store. Its high ceilings allow each store to stack merchandise right on the selling floor. This eliminates back room storage and inventory control problems.

In the wholesale distribution industry, driving costs down is critical to surviving. To operate at its low gross margins, The Price Club will purchase goods in huge volumes then resell them below the manufacturer's suggested retail prices.

Warehouse distribution appears simple, but is operationally quite complex. Each Price Club averages 24 annual inventory turns and $108 million in net sales. The purchase and movement of merchandise requires detailed planning, sophisticated data processing, and compatible logistics. The Price Club computers account for sales totaling $1,000 per square foot—15 times the volume of discount retailers.

Traits of Successful Warehouse Distribution

The secret to warehouse distribution is creating a balance between low distribution costs and fast inventory turnover. Traits of successful warehouse distributors include:

- *Rapid inventory turns.* Rapid inventory turnover is achieved through low prices on a limited number of stock keeping units.

- *Quality customer service.* The foundation for quality service is accessibility to large populations with inventory tied to market demand.

- *No interwarehouse shipments.* Merchandise shipped directly to warehouses from manufacturers eliminates interwarehouse logistics.

- *No emergency shipments.* Since merchandising does not adhere to regular buying practices, emergency shipments are not required.

- *Low inventory costs.* Since inventories turn every 16 days, capital is not tied up on goods, insurance costs, interest expense, pilferage, or product obsolescence.

- *High ticket items.* Profitability results from offering multiple packaged goods and large sizes.

MANUFACTURER WHOLESALE DISTRIBUTION

Reebok and Liz Claiborne both replaced independent wholesalers with their own forms of manufacturer wholesale distribution. Paul Fireman sells his Reebok, Weebok, Rockport, Frye, and Avia trademarks plus an assortment of apparel and accessories through his factory outlet retail stores. These outlets are located and operated away from retail traffic to minimize disruption in the normal distribution channels.

Liz Claiborne, on the other hand, jumped into the center of the retail scene with a collection of women's casual sportswear sold under a new label in its own stores. With its unique identity, First Issue specialty stores offer quality clothing by the same name. While its products are sold at prices generally lower than that of Claiborne's casual sportswear lines, First Issue actually competes with Claiborne for customers.

Through manufacturer wholesale distribution, Claiborne and Reebok undertake all of the distribution and wholesaling functions. They both saw this as the most effective way to reach their end users in certain markets.

Reebok and Claiborne products fit the conditions that favor this distribution channel. They are both financially strong manufacturers with long lines of high value perishables. Since Claiborne and Reebok also command large market shares, manufacturer wholesale distribution helps them sustain brand leadership.

Critical Success Factors of Manufacturer Wholesaling

Since manufacturers don't like to compete directly with retailers carrying their products, they tend to locate their outlets away from steady retail traffic. The vital functions of a manufacturer wholesale distribution strategy include:

- *Transportation.* Moving goods from manufacturing sites to the points of sale.
- *Inventory.* Holding goods between the time of production and the time of sale.
- *Promotion.* Persuading the market that the products meet their needs while not competing with established channels.
- *Transaction.* Cash, check, or credit card payment to transfer title for the goods.

CATALOG DISTRIBUTION

The Limited operates a 750,000-square-foot catalog distribution center for its mail order operation. It is home to Brylane, the second largest women's fashion catalog retailer in the United States. Brylane's five catalogs (Lane Bryant, Roaman's, Tall Collections, Lerner Woman, and Lerner Sport) each offer a distinct market focus.

Brylane's mail order distribution center is designed to provide the highest level of customer service. By placing the telephone at the center of its marketing mix, Brylane's staff of trained associates respond to customer needs and product orders 24-hours-a-day.

Victoria's Secret publishes 14 catalogs each year. With an extensive selection of intimate apparel, Victoria's Secret Catalogue Division features the same elegant lingerie brands as offered through its retail stores. Leslie Wexner tries to create a special fantasy with his Victoria's Secret Catalogues. The sexy pictures throughout the catalog help Victoria's Secret develop an identity all its own.

Leslie Wexner located his catalog and retail credit card operation in Columbus, Ohio. At this fulfillment center, more than 700 Limited "associates" handle its growing volume of mail order and telephone sales.

Benefits of Catalog Distribution

Catalogs deliver national and international markets through the nonwholesale distribution channel. This has become the vital link to the burgeoning at-home buying market. Its other significant functions in the marketplace include:

- Serves as an advertising medium
- Develops new customers where retail sites don't exist
- Facilitates new retail site locations among dense catalog zip code buyer penetration
- Reinforces brand imaging in retail locations.

VALUE-ADDED DISTRIBUTION

Businessland transformed computer distribution from an over-the-counter commodity service into a sophisticated value-added channel. David Norman combined service contracting and large volume discounting to create a global value-added distribution enterprise.

Norman pursued large corporate users, carved out vertical markets, configured networks, and offered complex software packages as part of Businessland's value-added distribution channel. Norman's ability to connect PCs to mainframes helped him secure prestigious Fortune 1,000 accounts. To configure and service these networks, Businessland hired systems engineers and technical support personnel at each store location.

Businessland became the largest seller of IBM PCs under IBM's "Customer Fulfillment Option" program. Corporate customers fulfilled their volume purchase agreements from IBM with computer purchases through authorized dealers such as

Businessland. The success of this program reflected the market's preference for value-added distribution when purchasing personal computers.

Businessland specialized in servicing multi-vendor environments. Its value-added approach solved complex problems of mixed-product configurations typically requiring networking expertise and support functions.

Earmarks of Value-Added Distribution

Value-added distribution can enhance other forms of product and service delivery. Consider the unique characteristics of value-added distribution and how to integrate it into other distribution channels:

- Retains more service technicians than sales personnel
- Provides extensive training and customer education
- Offers service calls during normal business hours
- Gives around-the-clock service support by phone
- Obtains performance and requirement input from clients
- Designs global support networks for multi-national clients
- Provides services for multi-vendor environments
- Sells a broad range of hardware, software, and supplies.

MULTI-CHANNEL DISTRIBUTION

Apple Computer delivers its products through a multi-channel distribution network. Its primary channel is a nationwide network of 2,000 authorized dealers. Value-added resellers (VARs) offer delivery into specialized vertical markets. Apple's national account direct salesforce targets both big business and government agencies. Apple also achieved distribution penetration through mail order companies.

Apple constantly searches out new ways to provide customers with sophisticated networking products and services.

For example, they created Academic Courseware in conjunction with Kinko's graphics. This program distributes university-developed Macintosh software through Kinko's copy shops to colleges and universities across the country. Apple even used its HyperCard technology to distribute information supplements on diskette.

Apple goes all out when it comes to distribution. They refuse to give up channels in exchange for exclusive arrangements. Apple's multi-channel distributors ship, bill, and collect for product purchases. They let dealers exchange product inventories within Apple's multi-channel network.

Apple gives customers plenty of distribution channels to choose from. They are especially effective in creating new channels for the education market. In one case, Apple appointed eight nationally recognized educators as Educational Technology Consultants. Their role was to prepare students for the twenty-first century by distributing and integrating Apple technology into the school systems.

Keys to Multi-Channel Distribution

In multi-channel distribution, customer demand is the key to success. Distributors stock what dealers sell and dealers sell what customers buy. These principles help build a strong multi-channel distribution network:

- Design and sell only top quality products.
- Offer distributors and dealers your standard margins.
- Use your marketing budget to drive customers to dealers.
- Teach distributors how to demonstrate your products.
- Provide technical support for your products.

OEM DISTRIBUTION

Manufacturers who design parts for inclusion in another company's products are part of the distribution channel known as

Original Equipment Manufacturers (OEM). While serving only a handful of major customers, OEM sales can total in the hundreds of thousands or millions of units.

Seagate Technology delivers nearly half of its disk drives through the OEM distribution pipeline. When the maturing personal computer market became price sensitive, Seagate produced high-performance disk drives for OEMs based on low prices. In the minicomputer market, Seagate provided rigid disk drives that emphasized performance. With mainframe and supercomputers, Seagate focused on reliability as a key benefit.

Seagate increased the size of its OEM channel with the acquisition of Imprimis Technology. The merger gave Seagate the broadest product line in the industry. It also added several major OEM customers to Seagate's existing distribution channel.

Seagate's OEM customers often place orders that fail to materialize, or defer delivery as a result of changes in their business needs. Such fluctuations have an adverse effect on Seagate's operations. So Seagate established nonexclusive agreements with dealers, resellers, and smaller OEMs to keep its distribution pipeline full.

Characteristics of an OEM Agreement

OEMs typically enter into purchase agreements with parts manufacturers. These agreements provide for volume discounts, order lead times, and product support obligations. Other terms and conditions include:

- *Quantity.* The master agreements typically do not commit the customer to buy any minimum quantity of products.
- *Deliveries.* These are scheduled only after receipt of purchase orders.
- *Length.* The agreements are entered into usually for up to two years, although product support obligations generally extend substantially beyond this period.
- *Cancellations.* With sufficient lead time, customers may cancel or defer most purchase orders without significant penalty.

INFORMATION DISTRIBUTION

Tele-Communications, Inc. distributes programming to nearly 15 percent of America's 40 million homes wired for cable. Its competitiveness results from its distribution efficiencies. TCI's distribution network encompasses a wide range of services that include satellite broadcasts, premium cable channels, shop-at-home channels, pay-per-view channels, and microwave common carriers.

Through strategic acquisitions, TCI became America's largest film distribution entity. TCI also participates in joint ventures to produce and distribute regional sporting events.

MCI also distributes information in the form of voice, data, and images over its telecommunications infrastructure. Its information distribution service has become a strategic asset and a competitive tool for customers. MCI is not just in the long-distance phone business. Its global distribution system makes it a major player in the world economy.

In its first year of hypergrowth, MCI had a $144 million information distribution infrastructure with one service that consisted of 7,800 network miles and served 40,000 customers. By the end of its hypergrowth decade, MCI had built a $6.9 billion distribution network with 60 different service options and 1.1 billion network miles that served 15 percent of the marketplace.

The Information Distribution Cycle

America's service economy is supported by a massive information distribution network whose lifecycle is depicted by a four-phase maturation process:

- *Investor phase* when a new information distribution network is put in place, before the information provides significant market value
- *Leader phase* when costs remain high but the information begins to create value for customers and distributors

- *Producer phase* when the service is perfected but the information costs are high due to lack of competition
- *Satisfier phase* when prices fall as competitors enter the market with new technologies.

LICENSED DISTRIBUTION

Computer Associates (CA) is a database management and applications software developer. Distribution is the key to its business success. Charles Wang believes that brilliant software designs are useless if potential customers cannot buy them due to poor distribution. CA overcame the problems that most software companies face when their products fall into niches that lack distribution.

Computer Associates' unique distribution methods, in fact, fueled its hypergrowth. CA does not sell or transfer title of its products to customers. Instead it licenses products on a "right-to-use" basis. Its licenses cannot be transferred or moved to other computer installations. CA even installs its systems on a trial basis, then provides a complete satisfaction warranty.

The company distributes its software through a one-time fixed-fee or a fixed-fee plus maintenance arrangement. Of CA's $1 billion in total revenue, nearly 25 percent comes from its maintenance fees. Its one-time license fees range between $2,400 and $637,000. For its microsoftware products, the license prices range between $49 and $7,495.

CA's strategy is to create a large distribution pipeline and always keep it filled. Following an acquisition, rebranded products are repositioned within the Computer Associates family and distributed by its worldwide salesforce.

Types of Licensing Agreements

In the computer business, the two basic mainframe software licenses include:

- *One-time fee and maintenance.* Under this arrangement, the customer pays a one-time fee plus an annual usage and maintenance fee that ranges from 13 to 20 percent of the one-time charge. The maintenance fee entitles the customer to receive technical support for the product and all enhancements to the product developed during the annual period covered.

- *Fixed fee.* Under this arrangement, the customer pays a fixed fee and receives the right to use the product for a specified term ranging from one month to three years. When the term expires, the license must be renewed in order for the product to continue in use. Maintenance can be part of the fixed fee.

AROUND-THE-CLOCK DISTRIBUTION

The distribution infrastructure has come under attack as a result of the hypergrowth phenomenon. Greater demands are now placed on manufacturers, wholesalers, and retailers as new technologies, new competitors, and new customers change the rules of the game.

Distribution requires greater flexibility and responsiveness to meet the demands of hypergrowth. The segmentation of the mass market created a new consumer value: *freedom of choice.* This freedom has expressed itself with the desire to order products, services, and information 24 hours/day, 365 days/year.

With this new-found freedom, the distribution sector of American enterprise has come under attack. The biggest casualties are proving to be those rigid distributors who cannot or will not provide customer-controlled delivery.

8

Never, Ever,
Run Out of Cash

T o achieve hypergrowth, you won't have the luxury of wait-ing a decade for your venture to develop. When your product or service succeeds, knock-offs and improved versions will appear on the market within a matter of weeks. In other words, hypergrowth occurs only if your company can mature quickly enough to avoid being swallowed by the competition.

Financing a hypergrowth venture requires more than just selling a dream. The key is to reduce the risks to your investors. The most important thing to remember when seeking investors is to show them how they'll get back their initial investment. When you can guarantee that your investors will get all of their money back first and minimize or eliminate their investment risks, you'll have plenty of backers.

Remember, some of the world's greatest products never got to market because the developers ran short of cash. Hyper-growth requires surplus capital to turn great ideas into great products and services. First and foremost, you must never, ever run out of cash. The flip side of this proverbial coin requires that you keep surplus capital on hand in order to seize new market opportunities. If you abide by these two rules you just might experience the thrill of hypergrowth.

RULE 1: NEVER, EVER, RUN OUT OF CASH

To fuel hypergrowth, learn how to raise capital at the lowest costs, at anytime, without hurting your company's credit ratings. In the end, running out of cash will cost you dearly:

- Two years after Paul Fireman purchased the North American rights to Reebok, he ran out of cash. So Fireman turned to Pentland Industries, an experienced footwear distributor, for help. In exchange for its $77,500 cash infusion, Pentland received 56 percent ownership of Reebok USA. Within six years, the value of Pentland's shares in Reebok grew to more than $600 million.

- After just one month in business, Fred Smith's accumulated losses totaled $4.4 million. After two years, Federal Express had $29.3 million in losses and Smith owed lenders nearly $50 million. On the verge of foreclosure, Smith was indicted for defrauding his bank, sued by his family, and replaced as president of his own company. Smith recapitalized Federal Express and his share of ownership fell from total control to just 8 percent, while investors grabbed 49 percent of the stockholdings.

- When Tax Reform dried up the demand for new tax shelters, Selig Zises moved Integrated Resources into the insurance business. To do so, he raised hundreds of millions of dollars through investment bankers. The combination of debt and the lack of customers caused Integrated Resources to default on nearly $1 billion of short-term notes and, shortly thereafter, declare bankruptcy. Remember, never, ever, run out of cash.

RULE 2: ALWAYS KEEP A CASH RESERVE

Hypergrowth offers fantastic opportunities for you to build up equity, fuel cash flow, or retire debt. To do so, you must build a cash reserve. This requires discipline and innovative asset management skills:

- The Price Club established a $250 million cash reserve that fueled its hypergrowth and reduced its costs simultaneously. With its war chest in place, Robert Price canceled his $30 million line of credit, then paid cash for land, buildings, and inventories during The Price Club's expansion.
- Five men from Joliet, Illinois, each pitched in $600 to start the Microwave Communications Company. After the "Joliet Five" ran into financial trouble, Bill McGowan came along and invested $50,000 of his own money to gain controlling interest in the venture that later became MCI.
- John Malone knew that the future of cable television required programming. So when Ted Turner ran out of cash, Malone jumped at the opportunity to make TCI a part owner of the Turner Broadcasting System. TCI gained access to TBS's 3,650 MGM/UA movie library, news and production studios. The $200 million investment was financed through TCI's existing credit facilities.

DEBT AND EQUITY FINANCING

Hypergrowth is funded through equity or debt financing, or a combination of the two. Debt financing involves funds borrowed by the business owner that are repaid with interest. Borrowing allows the owner to keep control of the business as long as no default occurs. Equity financing, however, is not repaid like a loan. Rather, it guarantees the investor a voice in the business and a percentage of future earnings. Consider the many debt and equity options available to fund your hypergrowth venture.

Before you start borrowing or giving up equity in your business, develop a set of pro forma financial statements. This will help determine your company's cash needs and the most desirable types of financing. Remember, the cheapest form of capital may not always be your best long-term financing strategy. From whom you raise money can be more important than the terms you negotiate.

PERSONAL FUNDS

The most common source of equity financing is personal savings. To invest personal funds in a venture demonstrates your level of commitment. Bob Magness, for example, started TCI when he sold off his cattle to raise start-up capital. He then moved TCI from Texas to Colorado, where he provided cable service to small towns in the surrounding regions.

While personal savings may be the most common way to finance a business start-up, not a single hypergrowth founder ever had enough money to fund their entire venture alone. Even Fred Smith, the son of a millionaire bus company owner, came up short of cash to launch Federal Express. When his father died, Fred Smith was left a $4 million trust. Following college, he bought controlling interest in Arkansas Aviation Sales. After turning around the unprofitable venture, Smith risked his entire inheritance (along with the trust funds of his sister and brother) on Federal Express, his overnight parcel delivery service. Even then, Smith found himself $50 million in debt after just his second year.

FAMILY AND FRIENDS

If you don't have enough money to start your hypergrowth venture, look to your family and friends for help. This is the cheapest form of equity and may be relatively easy to raise. Remember, when approaching anyone to back your venture, be a professional. Always provide a business plan that includes the risks and projected returns of your opportunity. A good way to deal with family and friends is to borrow a small amount, then repay the loan before seeking a second round of financing. The

Limited, with 3,095 units in nine different formats, actually started when Leslie Wexner borrowed $5,000 from his aunt to open his first store in Columbus, Ohio.

It is common for start-up companies to seek out capital from family and friends because their ventures are too new to provide lenders the collateral, cash flow, or track record they need to lend commercially. That is why Liz Claiborne invested $75,000 from personal savings, then borrowed an additional $180,000 from family and friends to start her fashion company.

PARTNERSHIPS

Another way to raise equity capital is through limited partnerships. In this case, the general partner is actively involved in the management of the business while the limited partners simply put up the money. In exchange for the capital, the owner gives up limited liability, limited management, and a share of the profits. The general partner is paid a management fee plus a percent of the gains, while the limited partners receive investment flexibility, flow-through tax benefits, and the investment returns.

Sol and Robert Price raised $2.5 million through a limited partnership when they opened The Price Club from a former aircraft parts factory in San Diego. The Price Club also expanded its operation to the Eastern Seaboard when 15 investors fronted 60 percent of the start-up money.

VENTURE CAPITALISTS

Venture capitalists offer equity to start-up ventures or high-tech companies facing risky futures. In exchange for capital, they will share in the ownership and hope to garner 3-to-5 times return on their investment within 5-to-7 years. In some cases, the returns come even faster and bigger. For instance, just two years after the Sevin Rosen Management Company invested

$2.5 million in the Compaq start-up, its stockholdings were valued at $38 million.

Venture capitalists tend to discard most proposals because they don't meet their investment criteria. The ones that do qualify for funding must then give up part ownership through common stock or convertible preferred shares. The founder usually keeps between 60 and 70 percent of the business . . . or less for a financially unstable venture.

Venture capitalists look for companies with superior management talent since this weighs heavily in hypergrowth success. Next, they try to differentiate the company from the competition to achieve product or service leadership in the market. Finally, they look to invest in growth industries that are not yet dominated by existing companies. You have the best chance with venture capitalists if you are a small, profitable company that can dominate a niche.

A word of caution when dealing with venture capitalists. They have ways to take control of your company should you not perform up to par. For example, an "event of election" clause lets venture capitalists elect a majority of directors; a "ratchet" clause increases the venture capitalist's share of equity if your company has to raise more money by selling cheaper stock; and a "negative covenant" can block you from raising money, issuing new stock, or amending bylaws without their permission.

Raise It Before You Need It

Compaq's strategy from the outset was to raise capital before it was needed. This let them operate without major financial constraints. During Compaq's first year, Ben Rosen helped raise an industry record of $30 million for the portable PC manufacturer. Rod Canion hosted Compaq's first investor meetings the day its prototype was unveiled. Immediately following funding, Canion laid the groundwork for subsequent rounds of financing.

Find Seed Money

Bernard Marcus turned to a group of high-powered investors to fund his Home Depot proposal. When Ken Langone, head of

Invemed Associates, put up $100,000 of his own funds, notable investors followed, including former astronaut and CEO of Eastern Air Lines, Frank Borman. These venture capitalists put up $2 million to launch the Home Depot. Bernard Marcus used this seed money to fine-tune his game plan and search the country for store sites.

Become a Professional Fundraiser

Bill McGowan knew that MCI was in the business of raising money. If he couldn't succeed in capitalizing his start-up, MCI would never place a single long distance call. So, McGowan broke MCI into 17 regional shell companies. His specialized long distance structure appealed to investors and McGowan raised $5 million in the first round of financing. With start-up funds in place, MCI received FCC approval for its design, which resembled television's local regulatory model.

WORKING CAPITAL

Capital is any form of wealth used to create more wealth. Technically speaking, working capital is your current assets less current liabilities. Accounts receivable and inventories are also considered part of your working capital. Companies use working capital to pay salaries, bills, and cover unexpected emergencies. When The Price Club introduced an annual membership fee of $15, its working capital increased by $2 million. The additional funds were used to further improve its gross margins.

Some hypergrowth companies use surplus working capital to fund expansion. Leslie Wexner, for example, financed The Limited's hypergrowth through internally generated funds. When The Limited undertook nearly $1 billion in capital additions for construction, renovations, equipment, and store expansion, it was principally funded by cash from operations. John Malone also leveraged TCI's billion-dollar cash flow to expand. He locked up programming and acquired struggling franchises. With the lifetime value of a cable subscriber estimated at $2,400, each new viewer Malone acquired added significant equity value to TCI.

INITIAL PUBLIC OFFERING

Companies that "go public" sell stock in their companies to investors. While this is an effective method of raising capital, it can also be expensive, time-consuming, and frustrating. A successful initial public offering convinces investors that your company can bring them a good return on their capital.

Once you decide to go public, the timing for your initial public offering (IPO) is critical. For instance, five years after its founding, Federal Express rode the momentum of air cargo deregulation into its IPO. That year, just 45 ventures raised a total of $250 million. Market conditions shifted and a decade later 541 offerings raised $24.2 billion.

It is not easy to take a company public since national underwriting firms rarely work with start-ups. In fact, they typically avoid initial public offerings for companies as small as Liz Claiborne. With only $79 million in sales, Claiborne somehow convinced Merrill Lynch to take it public. Ironically, Liz Claiborne turned out to be one of Merrill Lynch's most successful public offerings ever. The Claiborne launch opened at $19 a share and raised $6.5 million. Then the stock split 12 times in its first seven years as institutions grabbed up half of the 21.4 million shares. The founders, however, managed to keep $200 million worth of stock for themselves.

Don't Let Your Secret Out Too Soon

While investors wanted to take Home Depot public right away, Bernard Marcus kept his company private as long as he could. He knew that an inside look at its true success would spawn numerous Home Depot clones. Marcus finally bit the bullet and went public. Once Wall Street got wind of Home Depot's success, the company's profitability soared. Its stock split 3-for-2, then 5-for-4 just three months later. Home Depot then followed with a second public offering, which fueled a 160 percent increase in its stock price.

Sell Your Dream

Bill McGowan spent three years trying to raise enough money to establish his long-distance telephone network. McGowan was selling a dream because MCI was a non-operating business with zero income. Yet, his initial public offering sold 3.3 million shares at $10 each. Along with this $33 million, McGowan secured a $64 million line of credit. He also raised another $17 million privately. With $115 million in financing, McGowan transformed his dream into one of the wealthiest start-ups in the history of Wall Street.

Fuel Growth

Computer Associates had strong domestic and international growth as an independent software company. This track record made it easy for Charles Wang to take his company public. CA raised $3.2 million in its first round of public financing when it offered up 500,000 shares of common stock.

Create Wealth

When Wal-Mart went public on the NASDAQ Exchange, Sam Walton raised $3 million for his burgeoning discount business. Two years later, Wal-Mart switched to the New York Stock Exchange and hypergrowth fueled its stock growth. An original investment in 250 Wal-Mart shares, which sold for $4,125, was valued at more than one million dollars during its hypergrowth decade. Sam Walton discovered that he had many employees who earned more money from their stock dividends than they did from their paychecks. Many, in fact, had become multimillionaires from their appreciated stock.

For Leslie Wexner, his annual salary of $600,000 was dwarfed by the wealth created through his stock ownership. He earned $4.4 million annually in dividends from his shares of The Limited stock. In fact, during hypergrowth and before the market crashed, Wexner's personal fortune from appreciated stock exceeded $2.7 billion, qualifying him as one of the dozen wealthiest people in America.

STOCKS

The stock market is a great equity financing vehicle. To avoid debt financing and the impact of high interest payments on Federal Express profits, Fred Smith frequently tapped into the equity market. To finance 15 new 727-200F aircraft and a facsimile transmission network, Fred Smith looked to the stock market where Federal Express had raised $135 million in four previous public stock offerings. Smith's new issue caught a dramatic bull market that pulled the price of Federal Express stock up 50 percent and raised nearly $60 million.

Common stock provides investors ownership rights in a company. Shareholders elect the company's board of directors, who in turn, appoint top management. For investors, common stock is a risk-intensive investment vehicle. Yet, it offers the potential for huge rewards. The shareholder's return on common stock is a combination of dividend yield and the change in market price. The stock of most hypergrowth start-ups is classified as speculative, which means that the stock sells on the prospect of its future earnings rather than on its past accomplishments.

Boost Growth Rate

The Limited's stock carried a premium worth several billion dollars. Just halfway through its hypergrowth decade, 188 million shares of The Limited stock had a total market value of nearly $9 billion—three times its annual sales and 11 times its book value. The stock sold at 32 times its anticipated earnings, which fueled The Limited's growth for several years.

Add Equity

Reebok added $125 million in equity from a stock offering. With fresh capital, Paul Fireman aggressively pursued new product opportunities. As a result of his success, shareholder equity also increased from $89 million to $585 million in just two years.

Overcome Investor Fears

Compaq raised $66 million at the peak of high-tech public offerings. However, in its early hypergrowth years, Compaq's stock reacted unusually as it opened at 11, then bottomed out at 3½. Although Compaq's record sales brought it to the Fortune 500 faster than any company in history, its stock traded as low as $6.25 a share. Investors seemed leery of Compaq's hypergrowth, which came at the expense of profits. However, once Compaq overcame investor jitters, the stock climbed to record highs.

Keep Control

Bob Magness and John Malone sensed takeover pressures as a result of TCI's undervalued earnings. So they created a Class B Stock with 10 votes per share and swapped their A shares for B shares. Institutional investors were constrained for regulatory reasons from participating in this transaction. As a result, Malone and Magness came to control 60 percent of TCI's votes, while owning only 11 percent of its shares.

Find Lenders, Not Owners

Preferred stock is similar to common stock in that shares are issued in exchange for capital. Preferred investors are lenders, not owners, so they are not afforded the same voting privileges. Some preferred stocks are convertible and become common shares. Preferred stock is aptly named because it has priority over common stock on payments of dividends. Corporations appreciate the fact that dividends are predominantly tax exempt. Integrated Resources relied heavily on preferred stock for long-term financing of its ongoing cash shortfall. Preferred stock represented 70 percent of Integrated's total shareholder equity and became a cheaper financing vehicle than debt during its hypergrowth.

Sweeten the Pot

Similar to stock options, warrants offer investors equity in growing companies. Warrants are certificates that entitle the holder to acquire shares of stock at a certain price within a stated period. The warrant becomes common stock once its option to buy is exercised. Issuing warrants on common stock or bonds becomes an effective way to repay debts and balance your debt-to-equity ratio. Typically, a company that offers common stock to investors may increase the number of shares sold by including one warrant for every five common shares purchased. TCI's warrants brought big returns to its long-term investors. The Teachers Insurance & Annuity Association watched their $7.7 million in stock warrants grow to nearly $100 million during TCI's hypergrowth.

LINES OF CREDIT

One readily accessible form of debt financing is a line of credit. When you establish a line of credit, banks let you borrow, often up to 50 percent of your company's working capital, at any time. The line of credit is accompanied by a handling fee on the maximum credit amount plus interest on the amount borrowed. Since most companies need substantial amounts of capital to finance hypergrowth, they often negotiate huge credit lines to fund production during sales cycles. The credit line is then paid down as inventory and receivables are converted into cash.

Prepare for Seasonal Spurts

Cash generated by Reebok often exceeded its working capital requirements. Nonetheless, when bursts in market demand created a need for cash, Paul Fireman tapped his credit lines to finance manufacturing and stock inventories. As Reebok's product inventories increased from $380,000 to $123 million over a five-year period, Paul Fireman expanded his credit line from $30 million to $155 million to meet the demand.

Locate Cheap Capital

Access to affordable capital was a key element in TCI's hypergrowth. When John Malone's $77 million line of credit was approved, he used the money to refinance TCI's debt. During its hypergrowth decade, Malone expanded TCI's credit lines to $2.8 billion. He even secured international credit which gave TCI access to foreign capital pools at relatively low interest rates.

Watch Those Fees

With its $1.6 billion line of credit, The Limited paid millions of dollars in handling fees each year. So Leslie Wexner cut his credit lines in half to reduce the fees. However, The Limited kept its guaranteed $800 million Revolving Credit and Term Loan Agreement. Under this credit arrangement, banks were legally bound to lend The Limited up to the maximum agreed upon amount of money, as needed.

COMMERCIAL BANKS

At the heart of debt financing are commercial banks, who provide funds to be repaid with interest. They provide the greatest number and widest variety of loans. When a commercial loan exceeds a certain level, the business owner is required to provide security for the loan. In the case of Federal Express, Fred Smith Enterprise Company, Federal Express stock, and Fred Smith's personal assets secured its early bank notes.

When you apply for a loan, the lender will analyze your operating past, your current position, and your prospects for repaying the loan. For years, MCI teetered on the verge of bankruptcy. At one point, Bill McGowan actually owed his banks more than $100 million. The banks were so far committed that they could not abandon MCI without major financial repercussions. McGowan taught borrowers an important lesson through his trials: When you borrow a little bit of money, the bank is your lender. However, when you borrow a lot of money, the bank becomes your partner.

INVESTMENT BANKS

An investment bank is the agent between a company that issues securities and the public that invests in them. In exchange for a fee, investment bankers offer counseling, prepare documents, then sell and distribute securities. John Malone's gold telephone was a gift from TCI's investment banking firm, Drexel Burnham Lambert. Once Malone found a good investment opportunity, he simply called his investment banker and the deal was consumated and funded within hours. TCI's speed and its financial backing was a key to its hypergrowth success.

Integrated Resources also relied heavily on investment bankers to fund its up-front commissions and its high carrying costs. Drexel Burnham Lambert helped Integrated Resources build and sell new financial products with an infusion of $2 billion in high-yield, high-risk junk bonds and short-term commercial paper. Selig Zises returned the favor as one-fourth of Integrated's $2.3 billion insurance asset pool was filled with Drexel's unrated or below-investment-grade corporate bonds.

INSTITUTIONAL INVESTORS

With more than $2 trillion dollars in pension assets, institutional portfolio managers often invest in hypergrowth companies. Even after his exit from Apple, Steve Jobs continued to inspire investor confidence. When he started NeXT Inc., Jobs convinced major investors to buy in, including Canon and H. Ross Perot, founder of EDS and Perot Systems, who bought 16 percent of NeXT for $100 million. Investor performance, in this case, was a measure of how rapidly their invested capital appreciated.

High technology businesses offer institutional investors the potential of big returns. Yet, as institutional investors have discovered, it can be a roller coaster ride. Seagate Technology's stock, for example, tripled in value in one year. Then it dropped from 45 to 9 when earnings declined and production of disks drives was cut by 30 percent. Such a downward spiral was a major source of concern for Equitable Life, which held a 12 percent stake in the disk drive maker. To help boost institutional investor confidence, Alan Shugart personally purchased an additional 100,000 shares of the depressed shares.

INSURANCE COMPANIES

Individuals and corporations pay nearly $500 billion in policy premiums each year. This represents 8 percent of the U.S. Gross National Product. The total assets of the insurance industry is estimated at $1.8 trillion. Insurance company investment activities are carefully regulated by each of the 50 states in which they operate. With a policy loan, insurance companies let individuals borrow on the accumulated cash value of the policy. Insurance companies also use their huge cash reserves to finance shopping malls, office buildings, apartment complexes, and cable television enterprises.

To build a hedge against an uncertain financial future, TCI linked its capital sources and created a fixed-rate indebtedness of under 9 percent. TCI financed its assets from a variety of capital sources. These included $1 billion in new funds from banks and long-term notes, $615 million from insurance companies, $520 million from public debentures.

Federal Express depended heavily on insurance companies while it bled red ink. Fred Smith waited three years and four months from start-up to see his first profitable month. In the mean time, major insurance companies, including Prudential and Allstate, stood the gap for Federal Express. These companies (and other institutional and private investors) anted up a fresh $52 million so Smith could pay off previous creditors.

BONDS

A bond is an investment vehicle that is initiated with a contract called an indenture. This is a promise to pay a sum of money at a designated maturity date, plus periodic interest at a specified rate on the face value. Bonds come with different benefits to attract the different tastes of investors. For example, secured bonds use real estate and securities of other companies as backing while unsecured bonds, such as debentures, offer no specific security interest for repayment of the principle.

Bonds can have the features of both debt and equity. Convertible debentures are debt issues that can be converted to stock at a prearranged price for a designated period of time. Hypergrowth companies frequently offer this equity deal-sweetner to lure debt investors. Since part of the loan reverts to equity ownership and enhances the rate of return, the interest rates paid are often less than the rates that entrepreneurs must pay for debt financing.

Convertible subordinated debentures are a popular debt financing vehicle among hypergrowth companies. Seagate, for example, stepped up its R&D and acquisitions efforts following the introduction of the 3½-inch disk drive. It financed a 10,000-square-foot R&D facility in Boulder, Colorado, by issuing $250 million in convertible subordinated debentures. When Home Depot spent $34 million to acquire nine Bowater Home Center stores, $14 million was provided by issuing a 9 percent convertible subordinated debenture with a conversion price of $16.90. Compaq also offered a 5¼ percent convertible subordinated debenture on the New York Stock Exchange under the symbol CPQ 12. The net proceeds helped fund construction of its manufacturing facilities in Houston and Scotland.

ESOPs

An Employee Stock Option Plan (ESOP) is a way of obtaining capital from company employees. As a tax-driven benefit plan, funded by employees, companies with established ESOPs issue stock to an employee trust that is vested like a pension plan.

The terms under which the plan is administered afford qualifying employees the opportunity to purchase stock in the company at less than fair market value of the stock. This purchase can be in amounts proportional to their annual income.

Compaq reserved nearly 10 million shares of common stock for issuance under the company's employee stock option plans. Apple took its stock option plans even further by offering an Employee Stock Purchase Plan, a Savings and Investment Plan, an Employee Incentive Stock Option Plan, a Key Employee Stock Option Plan, and an Executive Long-Term Stock Option Plan.

TURN VALUE INTO CAPITAL

Several companies became financial innovators in order to fuel their hypergrowth. For instance, when faced with a cash shortage, Integrated Resources created a new financing technique called Accrual and Residual Receipt Obligations (ARROs). ARROs were repackaged long-term notes due from corporations occupying properties that Integrated Resources syndicated. Selig Zises simply adapted the investment banking technique of securitization to roll his long-term fee receivables into cash-generating ARROs. This accelerated his cash flow from frozen assets.

Liquidate Assets

MCI required millions of dollars a day in new capital to build its nationwide long distance network. Yet, after nearly two decades of litigation, Bill McGowan found himself in deep need of capital to keep MCI afloat. So he settled MCI's long-distance antitrust case with AT&T, then sold off his Airsignal division to raise a total of $233 million.

Shift Your Debt

When you sell a property and lease back the same space you can free up much needed real estate equity. This sale-leaseback arrangement shifts the mortgage debt to the landlord and off your company's balance sheet. After Bernard Marcus finessed Home Depot's sale-leasebacks, he was able to negotiate and obtain more debt and equity financing.

Fred Smith unveiled an ambitious capital-spending program that totaled more than $650 million annually for five years. While Smith paid for these investments with internally generated funds, proceeds from loan agreements, tax-exempt bond issues, and equity offerings, his corporate administrative facility was financed through a sale-leaseback arrangement.

HOW TO TAKE YOUR COMPANY PUBLIC

Selling stock in your company to the public is considered a right of passage in American business life. An initial public offering (IPO) serves as a status symbol and places value on your efforts in the marketplace. However, even more valid reasons to go public include:

- Fund the growth demonstrated by your market's demand.
- Build your company to a size that it won't fail.
- Reward key employees with stock options.

Step 1: Line Your Pockets

You must be prepared to invest about $500,000 in various professional services in order to take your company public—up to 10 percent of the stock proceeds on underwriter commissions. The brokerage house will charge you 2.5 percent of the value of the offering plus legal fees. Speaking of lawyers, count on them to extract about 10 percent of the net proceeds for their services. Accountants will charge about the same for their auditing and preoffering services. Then, your filing costs with the SEC will run about 0.02 percent of the maximum aggregate offering price. Blue Sky filings can range up to $15,000 per state. Be prepared to spend up to $50,000 to print your prospectus if it's a four-color package. The road show will cost another $50,000. Finally, you'll dole out $2,000 per month when your public relations firm starts promoting.

Step 2: Circle the Wagons

Find a reputable underwriting firm that can line up potential investors including institutions, brokerage houses, and retail customers. You will want to retain an underwriter that has a commitment to your industry and will promote your company to prospective investors. Key questions you'll be asked before they take your company public include:

- How much capital does your company really need and how will it be used?
- How do you know your company is ready to go public?
- What about your company will appeal to investors?

Step 3: Choose Your Weapon

You will most likely start out your public life on the NASDAQ Exchange, the second largest stock market in the United States. To get listed on the New York or American Stock Exchanges requires huge capital and operating resources that are generally out of reach for the start-up company. Some of the more popular IPO filings include:

- *S-1.* The basic filing statement that requires maximum disclosure in the initial filing and quarterly reports. This does not limit how much money you can raise.
- *S-2.* This lets companies without sales or business history file for a public offering.
- *S-18.* It authorizes generation of large amounts of capital without requiring a registration statement with the Securities Exchange Commission. It exempts limited partnerships and investment companies.

- *Regulation A.* This encompasses most start-up ventures and allows companies to omit forms 10-K, 10-Q, and 8-K from normal SEC filings if the business has fewer than 500 shareholders and less than $1 million in assets. It caps the offering at $1.5 million.

Step 4: Take the Show on the Road

Once your paperwork is completed, your underwriter escorts you around the country to drum up interest in your shares. This road show requires several presentations each day for about a week. IPO investors look for companies with at least $10 million in annual revenues, 10 percent earnings or better, a market niche with hypergrowth potential, a smart management team in place, a solid asset base, overseas opportunities, and proprietary products protected by patents. While IPOs are predominantly launched for manufacturing and high technology companies, many service niches are now providing good returns for investors.

Step 5: Prepare for the Morning After

Once you go public you are prohibited from selling your own shares for 90 days. This way investors don't have to worry about insiders withholding information, then dumping their shares before the news is uncovered. After your public offering, you will have your hands full with public disclosures, analyst inquiries, investor communications, proxy solicitations, annual meetings, media relations, and monitoring shareholder ownership.

Public companies must file reports with the Securities and Exchange Commission: 10-K is filed within 90 days of fiscal year-end; 10-Q quarterly filings must be submitted within 45 days of the end of the first three quarters of your fiscal year; 8-K report includes any significant changes in your company, from assets to management; 13-D lists any activity that would involve the buying of 5 percent or more of your stock; Proxy statements are required for shareholders meetings or to take a vote.

Going Public Isn't for Everyone

If you don't want the rigors of a full-blown IPO, you can still opt for a private placement. Regulation D's Rule 504 will let you raise up to $500,000 as long as you are not a public company, don't advertise for investors, and you file with the SEC within 15 days of your first sale. The key to a successful private placement is approaching individuals whose interest and expertise line up with what you are trying to do.

Most companies that attempt to go public and subsequently drop out, do so because the costs get out of hand; the tedium of drafting a prospectus becomes overwhelming; they don't want to disclose so many company secrets; or the long hours necessary to finish the IPO take away from running the business.

Finally, if you don't want to enter into the quarter-to-quarter demands of a public company, you can still raise millions of dollars bypassing the financial infrastructure of Wall Street. Private placements of debt or stock, joint ventures, strategic alliances, spinoffs of existing business units, or installment sales of your company are all ways to raise capital, stay private, and fund hypergrowth.

9

Fuel Your Hypergrowth

Once your first product or service succeeds and your cash flow is healthy, plan to introduce other offerings right away to fuel your hypergrowth. This is not as easy as it sounds; success has an intoxicating effect. You may find it tough to put aside the victory celebration and face uncertainty again.

Success also produces a myriad of challenges that include management training, technology investments, and new product development. To extend your hypergrowth curve, improve your current products by adding more features and benefits. Or bring out new products to enhance brand recognition. Or go for the innovative leap with an altogether new product or service. These strategies will help you recreate the hypergrowth rush.

Before you choose your follow-up strategy, step back and ask yourself if you're ready to go through another burst of hypergrowth. If you'd rather settle in and just manage your organization, you'll probably become too dependent upon your one hit product. You need to defend your territory and build upon your success. Remember that hypergrowth:

- Improves revenues and earnings
- Spreads your financial risk

- Expands your customer base
- Adds market share
- Diversifies product offerings
- Improves your product development cycle
- Draws in new management talent
- Extends your influence
- Exploits new business opportunities.

If you plan to fuel your hypergrowth through joint ventures or acquisitions, consider these words of caution: Make sure the commitment levels and strategic objectives of both parties are on the same plane. Don't overestimate your technology or underestimate your competition. Check that your distribution channels can handle a hypergrowth rush. Finally, be sure you have surplus capital backing to finance the inventory build-up.

When you target a company for acquisition, base its value on comparable public companies, or comparable private transactions, or the relative costs of starting the business from scratch versus buying the up-and-running company. Here are a few things you'll want to see in a viable acquisition candidate:

- Profitability
- Recurring revenues
- High growth
- Proprietary products
- In-house product development
- Direct salesforce
- International sales
- Market and technology leadership
- Strong management teams
- Financial reporting systems
- Audited financial statements

DIVERSIFICATION

Through diversification, your company can replenish its product line with new offerings. While a new product program provides hope for companies with low market share, they are also very risky. For example, more than 5,000 new supermarket products were introduced over a recent decade. Yet, only 93 of these products (2 percent) ever achieved sales of $15 million or more. If your diversification program is well-planned and makes strategic sense, it should produce a good return on investment.

Diversify or Die

Seagate Technology introduced the first 5 1/4-inch hard drive for personal computers. The device cut operating time by two-thirds and stored 10,000 typed, doubled-spaced pages, compared to only 170 pages on a floppy disk.

Although Seagate owned the 5 1/4-inch disk drive market, major computer manufacturers began integrating a new 3 1/2-inch disk drive. The smaller unit offered them more capacity and durability. The birth of the 3 1/2-inch disk drive spelled death to Seagate's disk drive dominance. Seagate needed to diversify or die.

Blindsided by the new technology, Seagate was forced to play catch up. Months behind its competitors in the 3 1/2-inch disk drive market, Seagate flexed its marketing and manufacturing muscles. They introduced 13 new products, six of those were in the 3 1/2-inch disk drive family. To speed up its diversification effort, Seagate invested $450 million to acquire Imprimis Technology, a leading manufacturer of 3 1/2-inch disk drives. This placed Seagate back on the cutting edge of a high growth market, the key to surviving in the disk drive industry.

Apply Old Knowledge to New Ventures

Diversification lets you apply lessons learned from the past to your current environment. For example, Leslie Wexner unveiled a new lingerie concept as part of The Limited family of stores. After just three years of operation, Victoria's Secret grew larger in total stores and dollar volume than The Limited achieved after 15 years. When Wexner diversified into his Superstore format, he provided triple the space of the typical Limited store. This allowed for greater shopping selection as entire brand merchandise lines were introduced simultaneously.

Look for Synergy

The Price Club made minor forays into real estate leasing and flea markets. However, its major diversification effort was The Price Club Industries. This division handled all processing operations including meat processing, photo processing, tire service, optical goods, pharmacy, and lens-grinding. The Price Club then established a research and development program to launch related manufacturing opportunities.

Create New Categories

Liz Claiborne positioned itself for hypergrowth through horizontal diversification. This fashion leader expanded across product lines and created new product categories. Claiborne moved from sportswear into active sportwear, into spectator clothes, into petites, into dresses, into girls' wear, then into casual wear. In making these moves, Claiborne focused on the various needs of the busy career woman. Finally, mens' wear was introduced carrying only the "Claiborne" name on the label.

Test New Formats

Sam Walton loved to test new retailing formats, especially those oriented toward discount merchandising, tonnage volume, and efficient distribution. Sam's Wholesale Club became Walton's most important diversification effort since discounting. Sam's grew from start-up to more than $7 billion in sales in less than seven years. This represented one-fourth of Wal-Mart's total sales volume. While Wal-Marts are established in suburban outskirts, Sam's metro marketing strategy placed warehouses right in the heart of large cities.

Sam Walton also diversified into a new merchandising concept, Hypermart*USA, a 200,000-square-foot "mall without walls," which included fast food and related services for one-stop family shopping.

Expand Product Lines and Distribution Channels

Reebok extended its hypergrowth through product and distribution diversification. Following its success in aerobics, Reebok designed shoes for basketball, the largest of all athletic footwear market segments. Paul Fireman simultaneously introduced three basketball shoe models based on extensive research of 21-year-old hoop stars.

Reebok diversified again by adding an infant shoe line called Weeboks. These tot shoes incorporated the latest technical advances for the special needs of infants. Weeboks expanded Reebok's athletic shoe distribution channels as family footwear shops, department stores, and specialty children's outlets carried the shoes. Reebok further diversified into tennis, running, conditioning, walking, golf, volleyball, cycling, casual & dress, children's, even mall-walking shoes.

Try New Materials

While working with a new adhesive, Reebok officials asked the Du Pont technicians to explore other polymer applications for its athletic footwear. Du Pont suggested incorporating plastic tubes, developed for the auto industry, into the soles of Reebok's ERS shoes. The flexible tubes gave the Reebok sneakers more bounce.

Paul Fireman then pushed Rockport, a division of Reebok, to introduce a women's shoe with invisible sports features. So the same technology used in a line of men's dress shoes was adapted to the woman's dress shoe. Reebok also provided a window in the sole of women's casual shoes so customers could view the built-in technology.

When Paul Fireman wanted to develop a revolutionary basketball shoe, he circumvented Reebok's bureaucracy. Fireman
retained a consulting firm to figure out how an intravenous
feeding bladder could fit into the instep of his basketball shoe.
The risky design, known as The Pump, created such a stir in the
marketplace, the shoe couldn't stay on retail shelves, even at
$175 a pair.

Broaden Your Product Base

When Paul Fireman purchased the Boston Whaler Company for
$42 million, it not only signaled a significant broadening of
Reebok's product base, it saddled Fireman with his first manufacturing operation. While Reebok had acquired several athletic
footwear and sportswear firms, the purchase of a power boat
company seemed far from its core business. However, the
Boston Whaler diversification was consistent with Reebok's
philosophy of being a consumer marketing company with an
upscale sporting goods image.

Seize New Opportunities

When Compaq diversified, its highest product objective was to
manufacture useful business tools that increased productivity.
Its computers typically offered more innovative features,
higher quality, and greater value than the competition. Compaq's decision to diversify into its 80386 chip technology before
IBM was based on the needs of the market, not on the moves of
its competitors. Rod Canion figured it would be unreasonable
to wait for IBM, especially if he could increase productivity
ahead of Big Blue. When Compaq seized the opportunity, its
engineers also got deeply involved in the chip design. This
broke down the traditional barriers between chip maker and
computer manufacturer.

Find New Ways to Pentrate the Market

Businessland helped corporations test state-of-the-art and top-
of-the-line products through Businessland Rents. With a myriad

of new products coming to market, Businessland let customers rent expensive computer systems before they bought. Due to the explosion in technology and its escalating costs, the market's motivations for renting soon expanded beyond setting up temporary locations and dealing with unplanned expansions.

ACQUISITIONS

Acquiring a business is a two-step process. The first step, buying it, is easy because that only takes money. The second step, running a profitable business following the acquisition, is tougher. Most acquisitions are accompanied by unforeseen changes in corporate culture that cause confusion and frustration among management and employees. Before your merger is completed, you will have to decide what to do with the name of the acquired company, its CEO, and its workforce. Computer Associates typically changes the company name, bids farewell to the CEO, then trims the workforce by as much as 40 percent.

Eliminate Competition

Charles Wang set out to build the largest independent software company in the world. Instead of taking years to develop new software, Wang simply acquired his competitors and their products. Of his 200 total software products, more than 150 came by way of acquisition. Through its distribution infrastructure, Computer Associates achieved rapid market penetration for its acquired products.

If Wang didn't have the software he wanted, he acquired it and built on it. Wang got everyone's attention when he paid $830 million to eliminate his biggest competitor, UCCEL Corp. It was a deal that sent shock waves throughout the software industry. By acquiring his biggest software foe, Charles Wang solved many problems associated with new product development, marketing, sales, and distribution.

UCCEL was just one of 18 companies that Wang acquired at a cost of $1.5 billion over a seven-year period. Following an acquisition, Wang's in-house software technicians enhanced the products and integrated them into the company's existing distribution pipeline. Wang typically capitalized and amortized each acquisition over five years.

Acquire Technological Leaders

Reebok entered the U.S. dress and casual shoe business by acquiring Rockport, a technological leader of high-quality, comfortable walking shoes. Paul Fireman paid $118 million for the Rockport Company, then he spent another $181 million to acquire Avia, his leading competitor in the high-performance athletic footwear market.

Scrap the Bells and Whistles

Following deregulation, John Malone put TCI's acquisition strategy into high gear. Malone waited for cable rivals to lose their shirts on state-of-the-art technology. When they were forced to sell out cheap, he snatched up their cable systems and replaced costly technology with "plain vanilla" systems. During Malone's three-year buying spree, TCI shelled out $3 billion to acquire more than 150 cable companies.

Avoid Confusion

IBM diminished PC price erosion when it placed a freeze on new dealerships. This forced Businessland to fuel its hypergrowth through acquisitions. David Norman bought the 36-store AmeriSources chain followed by his acquisition of MBI Business Centers. When the dust cleared, Norman had created the largest chain of company-owned PC retail stores in the United States. Not content with just the big business market, Norman then acquired ComputerCraft, Inc., a marketer of microcomputers, software, and accessories to the small business, professional, and home markets. Norman kept the ComputerCraft name to avoid confusion among Businessland's corporate clients and ComputerCraft's retail customers.

Consolidate Your Acquisitions

The Limited became the fastest-growing, most profitable specialty apparel retailer in the country through acquisitions in sports clothes (The Limited), fat clothes (Layne Bryant), young clothes (Limited Express), cheap fat clothes (Sizes Unlimited), catalog clothes (Brylane), and sexy clothes (Victoria's Secret). In his second year of hypergrowth, Leslie Wexner acquired Pic-A-Dilly, Inc. from Lucky Stores. The chain of 240 off-priced women's apparel stores had three buying and distribution centers that Wexner consolidated into a single operation. He then converted these stores into his Sizes Unlimited format. This created the largest off-priced women's apparel chain in the United States.

Form Strategic Alliances

Bill McGowan stunned the computer and telephone industries by forging a strategic alliance with IBM. MCI gave IBM 16 percent of its stock in exchange for Satellite Business Systems, its high-speed data transmission competitor. With the acquisition, MCI shed its maverick image and began to build upon IBM's reputation for quality. The Satellite Business System alliance also gave MCI the opportunity to hook up on national accounts marketing and learn what IBM's corporate customers needed from their phone service. As part of the strategic alliance, IBM offered MCI an option on an additional $400 million of convertible securities at rates 25 percent below the prevailing AA corporate-bond rate.

Buy Up Your Suppliers

Seagate Technology pursued a manufacturing strategy of vertical integration for its disk drive components. This meant that Seagate would build motors, disks, substrates, heads, printed circuit boards, and custom semiconductors. So Seagate began to acquire its suppliers, including Integrated Power Semiconductors Ltd. for $7.7 million. This Scottish company was a long-time Seagate vendor that made integrated circuits. Alan Shugart then paid $4 million for Aeon, a California-based Seagate supplier of substrates used to make thin film magnetic recording media.

Don't Mix Oil and Water

Union-free Federal Express approached the acquisition of unionized Tiger International with caution. The merger nearly shattered the spirit that Fred Smith had worked so hard to build. Ballot-burnings and harranguings were commonplace occurences. Smith tried to persuade Tiger pilots that it would be easier to vote a union in than to vote one out. So he created the "Let's Give It A Year" campaign and the union went down in defeat by a 3-to-1 margin. The day Tiger International became part of Federal Express, its unions were decertified.

DIVISIONALIZATION

Reorganizing an operation into separate divisions helps focus attention on the needs of each operating unit. To accomodate Reebok's tremendous growth, Paul Fireman reorganized his company into three divisions—footwear, apparel, and international—each run by a division president. Reebok International was further split into two units to focus separately on the fashion and performance markets. These moves cut the company's new product development time by half. Since fashion is a fast moving industry, Reebok's flexible structure kept it in step with the market.

Align with the Market

Computer Associates established a new organizational structure when Charles Wang divided it into four divisions—Applications Products, Systems Products, Micro Products, and International Products. Wang's divisionalized company paralleled the evolving software marketplace.

Cope with Global Demands

Apple Computer restructured itself into four divisions—Apple USA, Apple Europe, Apple Pacific, and Apple Products. This new structure helped Apple stay flexible and responsive as a multi-billion dollar global enterprise. Its four divisions, which operate independently, are headed up by separate division presidents.

Apple USA establishes new distribution channels and develops corporate-wide information systems. Apple Europe, which includes European, African, Mediterranean, and Middle Eastern countries, allows each subsidiary to function independently, based on the economic or cultural requirements of the region. Apple Pacific was created to strengthen the Australian, Canadian, and Japanese markets, and to pursue emerging opportunities in the Far East and Latin America. Apple Products designs future hardware and software architectures. To help accelerate its new product development process, Apple Products purchased a $16 million Cray Supercomputer.

Stay Close to Change

Although divisionalization indicates a traditional pathway to continued growth, Liz Claiborne committed to a nontraditional management structure. Claiborne divisionalized its marketing activities to establish closer customer contact. This helped Claiborne stay on top of its customers' new fashion requirements. Claiborne's 13 divisions came to include: Liz Claiborne Collections (sportswear), Lizsport (sportswear), Lizwear (sportswear), Liz Claiborne Petites (sportswear), Liz Claiborne Dresses, Liz Claiborne Petite Dresses, Liz Claiborne (larger sizes), Claiborne (menswear), Claiborne (furnishings), Liz Claiborne Accessories, Liz Claiborne Cosmetics, Dana Buchman, and First Issue (retail stores).

Demand Profitability

Leslie Wexner restructured The Limited corporation into different divisions with the parent company providing a support staff. Division presidents were given the necessary resources to meet Wexner's mandate for profitable growth. He then turned them loose to penetrate their markets.

Rekindle the Entrepreneurial Spirit

Bill McGowan overcame MCI's lethargy when he created seven divisions, similar to the structure of the seven Regional Bell Operating Companies. This not only gave MCI a chance to keep a closer eye on its Bell competitors, but rekindled MCI's entrepreneurial spirit. Each division performed the same functions and maintained absolute authority over its profits and losses.

McGowan cross-pollinates regional creativity through his MCI Audits. Audit groups consist of a customer service supervisor, an on-site supervisor, and the branch manager. Each month, regional representatives visit the headquarters of another region for a two-day look around. McGowan involves himself in the audits when long-term planning is part of the agenda. Auditors spend the first day studying how their counterparts handle the same job. The second day is devoted to sharing observations and generating options for improvement.

Don't Grow Too Big, Too Fast

Tele-Communications, Inc. had become too big and too powerful after just three years of deregulation. And Congress was not going to let it grow any bigger, either vertically or horizontally. In response to mounting pressures from Capitol Hill and Wall Street, TCI prepared to break itself into separate programming and cable companies. Since TCI's spin-off plan was voluntary, it took the steam out of most legislative initiatives. TCI put several operating contingencies in place. However, John Malone wouldn't reveal his new company structure until the new rules for cable were on the table.

DOMESTIC EXPANSION

Successful hypergrowth expansion requires tight control over operations, high product or service acceptance, new site availability, absence of direct competition, and minimal market saturation. To kick hypergrowth into high gear with saturation marketing, stores are clustered tightly in high traffic areas. While this tends to cannibalize some sales, saturation marketing virtually eliminates the need for advertising. It makes stores easy to supervise and draws customers away from the competition. Finally, expanding in clusters can extend brand identity for hypergrowth companies and their products.

Grab Market Share

The Price Club expanded with multiple stores in the same markets. Robert Price didn't care about market growth since his hypergrowth was fueled by sales taken from competitors' market share. Its domestic expansion required a strong wholesale foundation to support new warehouses. So The Price Club expanded into markets where large numbers of small businesses of 30 to 50 employees existed.

Roll with the Punches

With rapid domestic expansion, Liz Claiborne came to expect new market challenges. When she introduced children's clothes, the scaled-down version of her women's line proved too sophisticated for youngsters. Claiborne redesigned the look and overcame the problems. Then she discovered that children's stores separated clothes by size rather than by price: $25 LizKids overalls hung next to $10 duds. So Claiborne worked closely with retailers to establish separate LizKids shops.

Guard Your Culture

Home Depot took great pains to prevent dilution of its corporate culture. When Bernard Marcus expanded from Atlanta into the Northeast, he relocated dozens of committed employees to head up different departments. Marcus moved managers, assistant managers, and many hourly workers hundreds of miles to ensure that the new stores were run by those bred in his Home Depot culture.

Expand at Your Own Pace

While its competition announced grandiose expansion plans, The Price Club would not risk its management quality to grow beyond its capacity to manage. Robert Price expanded only when the time was right and the management was in place, not because Wall Street expected it of him. While analysts expressed impatience with his measured pace of hypergrowth, Price refused to be rushed.

Penetrate Your Market

Fred Smith's expansion of Federal Express was so pervasive that it became the first corporation in history to cross the billion-dollar barrier within a decade of continued operations. To further penetrate its market, Federal began delivering more low-margin letters than profitable parcels. Fred Smith quickly refocused on handling packages that weighed up to 150 pounds, where service took precedence over price. Federal Express again extended service with its Saturday pick-up and delivery.

Federal Express also gained market share when it enlarged its aircraft fleet with 727s, increased capacity at its Memphis Superhub, and added its Newark and Oakland Metroplex operations. Fred Smith then created a network of Business Service Centers where customers dropped off the packages themselves. Free-standing, drive-through kiosks in office parks and major shopping centers also improved Federal's penetration in established markets.

Test New Technologies

MCI gained ground on AT&T when it created a facsimile network to deliver condensed reports from Gannett's *USA Today* newspaper. The service provided information on demand through two delivery systems. One sent out summaries a day before the paper was published while the other used payer-calls 900 numbers to provide selected information. When readers called specified numbers from a fax machine, codes on the telephone pad were punched and specific information, such as financial reports or sports scores, were faxed back.

The idea of sending specially tailored information by fax became a powerful marketing tool for companies outside the newspaper industry. Catalog retailers, for example, adapted the concept to deliver time-sensitive information on its products. Brokerage houses used it to deliver customized information for investors.

Stay Close to Your Trendsetters

During Home Depot's hypergrowth, Bernard Marcus expanded his company into California with nearly a dozen sites. Considered the largest do-it-yourselfer state, The Home Depot's California operation had its own real estate, advertising, and merchandising departments. Management services were actually duplicated in the Atlanta home office and in Fullerton, California, to give the West Coast operation better control over the huge market. The bicoastal operations keep in close contact through Home Depot's satellite network system. Computer-to-computer communications and video transmission let top management review sales figures and discuss market developments directly with personnel at each store site.

INTERNATIONAL EXPANSION

International expansion is a way to grow without placing added brand pressure on your domestic products. It also acts as a hedge against a declining U.S. dollar. When products are denominated in U.S. dollars, your cost of sales decline as the dollar drops against foreign currencies. Further, if your royalties are based on manufactured costs as stated in U.S. dollars, they also rise as production costs increase. Exports done by letter of credit also mean that your money is in the bank once you ship the merchandise. If your domestic sales slow, market share slips, or profits decline, international expansion is a viable way to inject rapid growth back into your venture.

Learn the Languages

Apple achieved rapid global expansion primarily because it overcame the international language barriers. Apple's product lines became available in Japanese (KanjiTalk), Chinese (ZhongwenTalk), Korean (HangulTalk), French Canadian, Thai, Spanish, a local English version for Australia, plus 18 different European languages.

Grow the Market

Compaq became one of the first personal computer dealers behind the Iron Curtain when it created a network of 13 private computer dealers in East Germany. Compaq aggressively penetrated Europe, Southeast Asia, Australia, and Canada before the close of its second year of business. By expanding internationally, Compaq helped grow these markets on its products.

Provide Continuity

Businessland found that multi-national corporations wanted the same supplier to provide hardware and systems integration worldwide. So David Norman developed computer chains in the United Kingdom, Canada, and Japan. Its Tokyo office was backed by five major Japanese corporations who gave Businessland contracts, while Businessland reciprocated with one-stop service and network support.

Get in Early

The foreign athletic shoe market, while more than three times the size of the U.S. market, is several years behind in its maturation. Paul Fireman projected that offshore sales would soon provide half of Reebok's revenues, up from 5 percent during its hypergrowth decade. Reebok grew internationally through brand-name acceptance across foreign borders and centralized global retailing practices. Reebok, for example, signed Russian tennis star Alexander Volkoff to promote its products through-out the Soviet Union.

Develop an Infrastructure

As the express delivery business in the United States slowed and competition increased, Fred Smith looked internationally to extend his hypergrowth. Smith first acquired a number of local delivery companies. Then he paid $880 million for Tiger International to create the world's largest air-cargo company. In just three years, Federal Express expanded service into more than 100 countries.

Several other acquisitions enhanced Federal's expansion into foreign markets. In Canada, Smith purchased Cansica, Inc. Then Federal Express acquired Lex Wilkinson Ltd., which gave it total coverage of the United Kingdom, France, and West Germany. The Williams Transport Group acquisition also gave it complete coverage of the British Isles. Finally, Federal's Far East operation came to include service in Hong Kong, Japan, Singapore, Australia, and New Zealand.

JOINT VENTURES

Joint ventures are independently managed and financed 50/50 partnerships. TCI entered into joint ventures with TKR (Knight-Ridder), TCI-Taft, Lenfest Communications, and Bresnan Communications. TCI's joint venture participation is through representation on boards of directors and various committees.

Become a Team Player

Businessland teamed up with a Big Six accounting firm to joint venture systems integration projects. The partnership gave Businessland a foot in the door with corporations owning large, complex information systems. Businessland provided local area network expertise while the accounting firm provided applications development and strategic systems planning.

Businessland also sold, implemented, and supported its micro-computers, local area networks, and gateways.

Pool Your Resources

Liz Claiborne entered into a joint venture with Avon, Inc. for a line of fragrances. The 50/50 partnership, called Liz Claiborne Cosmetics, was also Avon's first foray into retail. This joint venture was organized through three licenses. The first provided for 50 to 100 years of a joint venture partnership in which Liz Claiborne, Inc. and Avon, Inc. held 50/50 ownership, and split the profits equally. The second license left the final decision-making power for marketing to Liz Claiborne Cosmetics. The third phase of the agreement was a renewable three-year service contract for development and manufacturing to take place at Avon.

Liz Claiborne also joint ventured with a developer for the construction of its warehouse/distribution/office facility. The venture totaled $22.5 million in capital expenditures with $8.5 million used to equip the facility and expand Claiborne's showroom.

Find a Tour Guide

The Price Club expanded into Canada through a 50/50 joint venture with Steinberg, Montreal. They planned to undercut supermarket prices by 12 percent and department store prices by as much as 37 percent. The partnership capitalized $200 million over five years to build a Canada-wide chain of The Price Clubs.

Look in Your Own Backyard

Apple computer matured into a multi-national corporation then formed joint ventures with companies within its own industry. Apple and Digital Equipment Corporation (DEC) created a joint venture program to integrate their respective networking environments. In addition, DEC became an authorized service provider for Apple products at selected sites.

Apple and Texas Instruments also announced the MicroExplorer Computer System. This product consisted of an Apple Macintosh II equipped with Texas Instrument's Explorer Lisp co-processor and advanced software. It became one of Apple's largest value-added resellers for the Macintosh computer.

One of Apple's most important joint ventures occured early in its formation when Visicalc designed its software program for the Apple II. Visicalc's electronic spreadsheet helped Apple penetrate small and large businesses alike. In many cases, the Apple was sold on the strength of the Visicalc software.

LICENSING

For any company that has made a name for itself, licensing is a great way to expand. The fundamental criterion for accepting a licensing arrangement is its ability to enhance your product line's value. New markets may also open up through licensing with selected manufacturers. However, before you enter into a licensing agreement, tap the full potential of your current business opportunities.

Keep Tight Controls

In the second year of its hypergrowth decade, Liz Claiborne entered into licensing arrangements with Kayser-Roth for dress hosiery, the U.S. Shoe Corporation for footwear, and Burlington Industries for home products such as bedsheets, pillowcases and bath towels. Claiborne also had licenses for eyewear and optics. Licensees created specially designed and approved products under the Claiborne trademark. Although it collects up to 10 percent of the net sales against a guaranteed minimum royalty, Claiborne goes to great lengths to protect its name and image. Claiborne even voided a contract with a licensee who continually ignored its advertising and marketing policies.

Pay Now or Really Pay Later

IBM turns up the heat on its emerging competitors by aggressively enforcing its 10,000-patent portfolio. When IBM challenged Compaq's use of certain patented technologies, Compaq paid out more than $100 million over five years to avoid infringement penalties. IBM typically collects between 1 and 3 percent of total revenues for its licensing rights.

INVESTMENTS

An investment is considered an ownership interest of less than 50 percent in another venture. For TCI, its investments in affiliates generally account for between 20 and 50 percent of the company's voting interest. TCI carefully analyzes each investment candidate. John Malone knows that expensive technology can suck profits dry. Generally, the larger the portfolio of technology, the lower the return. A safe investment for TCI is a high-market share company with low-technology intensity.

Buy Rather Than Build

TCI prefers to buy into a business rather than start it from scratch. John Malone finds that an up-and-running business, even though unprofitable, can at least offer TCI a tax shield. Malone doesn't mind providing cash infusions and distribution channels if the struggling company shows potential for future profits.

Look for Value-Added Investments

Tele-Communications, Inc. has cable systems in 47 states and extensive investments in more than 35 programming companies. As a result of its investments, TCI evolved from a pure cable television company into a fully integrated cable-programming-distribution entity. John Malone knew that cable television was driven by programming. So he strength-ened his programming inventory with equity investments in Cable Value Network (CVN), Black Entertainment Television, Inc. (BET), the Discovery Channel, Turner Broadcasting Systems, Inc. (TBS), the American Movie Classics Company (AMC), and many more.

Broaden Your Audience

TCI invested $5 million in the Video Jukebox Network, a fledgling pay-per-view operation that lets viewers select music videos they want to watch by calling a 900 number. TCI's equity investment boosted Video Jukebox's growth and increased its distribution.

Invest in Pioneers

The popularity of compact disks created a big demand for digital music services. When TCI surveyed its subscribers, two-thirds said they would pay at least $7.50 per month for such a service. TCI invested in International Cablecasting Technologies to create the Digital Music Network, which offered eight commercial-free music formats. The unique technology compressed digital sound onto a video signal that was transmitted via satellite to cable systems with no loss of sound quality. A special device then split off the audio signal into the digital tuner of a subscriber's stereo system.

Invest in Value

Compaq invested $12 million in Conner Peripherals, Inc., a disk drive supplier, during its development stage. Compaq received about $30 million in pretax gains from increases in the carry value of the investment in Conner. The gain resulted from Conner's issuance of additional securities at prices higher than the per share carrying value of Compaq's interest in Conner. Three years later, the market value of Compaq's investment in Conner was $150 million on the NASDAQ Exchange.

When Compaq invested $21 million in mutual funds holding Adjustable Rate Preferred Stocks, it realized gains of $352,000 upon liquidation of a portion of the investment. Together with the tax advantages from the investment, Compaq's earnings on an adjusted basis were higher than the yield from more conventional investments.

WEIGH YOUR RISKS AND REWARDS

To fuel your hypergrowth, you must invest your resources where they will return a profit. With risky "growth-at-all-costs" strategies, the first bump in the road can be a bone-jarring experience. You need to weigh the risks and rewards of each strategy in order to fuel your hypergrowth.

Establish Checkpoints

After you've committed to diversify with a new product, conduct additional research to determine the market's receptivity and product viability. Next, reassess the product with engineering, finance, manufacturing, and marketing before you fund production. With all costs on the table, establish a realistic selling price. Then re-evaluate the opportunity in light of its sales and profit potential. While such checkpoints may seem like overkill, they will safeguard you against manufacturing a product that has no reality in the marketplace.

Clarify Your Goals

When you go looking for an acquisition, start with the unique characteristics of both the acquirer and the acquiree. Then make sure the goals and strategies for both are the same. Federal Express, for example, was an industry "retailer" that delivered small packages door-to-door. It acquired Tiger International, a "wholesaler" that delivered heavy cargo from airport-to-airport. Federal Express soon learned the difference between wholesale and retail express deliveries from The

Limited. As a Tiger customer, The Limited evolved into the world's largest air-freight shipper over the Pacific. To accomodate its delivery demands, Tiger International established a hub in Columbus, Ohio, home of The Limited's distribution center. Following the acquisition of Tiger, Federal Express closed down the Ohio hub to consolidate Tiger's Midwest operation in Indianapolis. Within weeks, express service to Columbus became unpredictable and The Limited took its $60 million account to another delivery company.

Accelerate Your Pace

While caution is the watchword for diversifications, and compatibility is a key criterion for acquisitions, speed is the vital component that congeals your hypergrowth. Accelerating your pace of business can improve sales, service, profitablility, and market share. When you package speed as a customer benefit, you'll improve the quality of your everyday operation. Spot opportunities to accelerate your operation and gain an edge over the competition. When you learn to make decisions quicker, develop products earlier, and fill orders faster, you'll find yourself in the fast lane to more hypergrowth.

10

Expect the Unexpected

Hypergrowth may come quickly, but it never comes easily. Its path is filled with hundreds of roadblocks. These unexpected events represent the biggest potential barriers to hypergrowth:

- If you get fired from your job
- If your business plan sputters
- If your product design differs from the market demand
- If you lose your biggest account
- If your earnings collapse
- If you get sued
- When your competitors wise up
- If your legislators wreak havoc
- If fatigue sets in.

Hypergrowth executives overcome unexpected events because they are first and foremost winners. They display an uncompromising commitment to dominate. Refusing to be stopped by external forces, they garner the necessary resources to snatch victory from the jaws of defeat. Even though they'll experience setbacks, hypergrowth executives always stay focused on their big picture opportunities.

Expecting the unexpected requires flexible planning and a resiliant management structure. Successful hypergrowth executives respond similarly when faced with unexpected events. They tend to:

- *Stay positive.* Convinced they can weather any storm, they view unexpected events as a personal challenge.
- *Seek help.* Since no executive can solve every problem alone, they find the most qualified specialists to help define the nature of the threat.
- *Gather the facts.* Whether they get sued or their earnings collapse, hypergrowth executives gather all the facts, study all the options, then design the best strategy to counter the threat.
- *Communicate clearly.* Hypergrowth executives share the unexpected event with management, then gain input regarding a strategy's impact on employees and customers.
- *Act decisively.* Hypergrowth leaders adjust their tactics quickly when early feedback differs from the anticipated outcome.
- *Celebrate victory.* When the threat has been crushed and victory declared, these leaders take time to congratulate all those involved.
- *Stay prepared.* A short summary of what they did to gain victory is recorded for future reference.

Principle: Winners never quit, and quitters never win.

IF YOU GET FIRED

Getting fired can be a traumatic life experience or the opportunity to pursue your hypergrowth dream. The first thing to do is turn negative emotions into a positive plan. Start by answering the big question, "What do I really want to do?" Then pull out your rolodex and begin stirring up interest in your own venture.

Hypergrowth executives who were fired from jobs always pursued something bigger than anything they had ever known before. So, stay positive, always keep a back-up plan handy, focus on solving big problems, and look for new opportunities.

Keep a Back-Up Plan

Bernard Marcus migrated to the world of retail from his training as a pharmacist. While managing a Handy Dan home center store in Southern California, Marcus experimented with a variation of the chain's retailing concept. He tested the combination of low prices, high volume, and quality service. Marcus noticed that when prices were discounted, sales volumes increased, and costs, as a percentage of sales, decreased.

Bernard Marcus shared his findings with an investment banker named Ken Langone. Langone was so impressed with Marcus and his operation that he purchased 500,000 shares of Handy Dan stock. Langone's investors were also impressed as their Handy Dan stock produced a six-fold return.

Without warning, Marcus was fired by Sanford Sigoloff, a corporate turnaround specialist who was hired to reorganize Handy Dan's parent from bankruptcy. Five days later, Marcus contacted Langone and asked him to consider backing a full-scale version of his Handy Dan retail experiment. Langone gathered a group of investors, lawyers, bankers, and real estate executives to discuss the new venture. At that meeting, they raised $2 million to help launch the industry's first warehouse home center chain called Home Depot.

Stay Focused on Problem-Solving

Sol Price, son of a union organizer, grew up in San Diego and attended USC law school. He developed a thriving corporate law practice, but was more intrigued by business than law. In fact, he often negotiated for equity in the companies he represented in lieu of his legal fees.

Price then started FedMart, a no-frills, cash-and-carry merchandise and supermarket chain. FedMart's annual sales soon exceeded $300 million. After FedMart went public, Price looked for ways to take the company private again. He discussed his plight with Hugo Mann, a West German businessman. Mann, who had built a $1.5 billion discount department store empire, proceeded to purchase 75 percent of FedMart's shares.

Price remained FedMart's president, but answered to Mann. Although the loss of control distressed Price, he became incensed when the German retailer changed the FedMart formula by advertising extensively and using loss-leader items to attract shoppers.

Tensions ran high during the first seven months of the relationship. Then, at the second board meeting, Price pulled Mann aside and pleaded with him to sell the company back. Instead, Mann fired Price and changed the lock on his door. After a series of lawsuits, a court ruled that Price was unfairly fired and Mann had to pay Price his $125,000 annual salary for the next five years.

The firing was a low point in Sol Price's life. Over the following months, Sol took long walks with his son, Robert, who worked in the family business. Father and son concluded that small businesses had everything going for them except they couldn't buy right. They committed to finding a solution to this problem.

During those long walks, a warehouse operation they had visited in Holland became a frequent topic of conversation. While not terribly impressed by the company, something about the concept led them to sell shares in a new venture that became The Price Club. They raised $2.5 million and opened the original discount warehouse membership club in a former aircraft parts factory.

Look for New Opportunities

The more Apple Computer grew, the less Steve Jobs enjoyed his work. Not cut out to run a big organization, Jobs recruited John Sculley from the Pepsi-Cola Company to become Apple's new president. Shortly after Sculley arrived, things soured for Jobs. His founding partner, Steve Wozniak, left to pursue a new video venture. Then, with costs rising, Sculley laid off 1,200 Apple employees. Confrontation between Sculley, Jobs, and the board of directors found the board siding with Sculley. Jobs departed and moved on to start his NeXT computer company.

Principle: Adversity carries the seed of a greater opportunity.

IF YOUR BUSINESS PLAN SPUTTERS

In business, it is not a matter of making mistakes that counts; it's how well mistakes are handled that dictates who enters into hypergrowth. Research, analysis, and planning aside, only a business plan's implementation can reveal whether it will succeed or sputter. When a business plan sputters you can make early adjustments to the plan or wait until the market turns.

Adjust the Plan

Charles Wang tells his programmers at Computer Associates that they must "own" the products with which they work. He expects them to write the software, position it, support it, implement it, and distribute it.

Wang teaches his staff to find the quickest way to market. He urges his employees to make decisions and tolerate mistakes as long as they become learning tools. Workers are trained to be productive and carry their own weight.

However, when an in-house software development team misses its deadline, Wang yanks people off, leaving a skeleton crew to finish the work. Wang holds to the notion that a late project can be speeded up by reducing the number of people working on it. He typically reassigns the two weakest programmers from a staff of eight. This lets the stronger six move faster because they no longer have to oversee or redo the work of others.

Wait until the Market Turns

Paul Fireman knows what it feels like for a business plan to
sputter. At 32, he took over a family distributorship for fishing
tackle equipment. He watched the business go sour when manufacturers began dealing directly with retailers. Searching for
new business opportunities, Fireman spotted an unusual running shoe while attending a trade show. He negotiated with a
closely held English company for the U.S. rights to manufacture
and distribute Reeboks.

Fireman began offering the most expensive running shoe on
the market to a largely indifferent audience. He spent two-
thirds of his day going from store to store selling shoes. Then
he'd return to the warehouse to inspect, pack, and ship his daily
orders. Although Fireman's offerings aroused curiousity among
retailers, the shoes didn't sell well.

After two years of flat sales, financial problems beset Fireman. He turned to Pentland Industries plc for help. In exchange for a $77,500 cash infusion, the British shoe distributor
obtained 56 percent ownership of Fireman's U.S. operation.

The unresponsive market spurred Fireman to study his
targeted consumers more closely. He and his staff would stand
for hours in shoe stores observing how athletes handled shoes
and how they reacted to the styles. Fireman recorded every
question consumers posed. Out of this basic market research
emerged Reebok's revolutionary concept to combine fashion
and function.

With the competitive running-shoe market saturated, Fireman gambled that aerobics would be the next wave of athletic
endeavor. So he designed an aerobics shoe for fashion-
conscious women who had the performance requirements of
athletes.

For the first three months, it looked as if Fireman's business
plan was going to flop again. Sales were stagnant. But in the
fourth month sales began to soar . . . and they never came
down. Annual revenues more than doubled each of the next
three years—$1.5 million to $3.5 million to $13 million. In the
following two years, sales increased by 500 percent to $64

million and $300 million. Sales then tripled to $900 million
just 12 months later.

Principle: When you fail to plan, you plan to fail.

IF YOUR PRODUCT DESIGN DIFFERS FROM THE MARKET DEMAND

Hypergrowth results when a new product strikes a responsive
chord with customers. Successful products frequently emerge
from extensive market research and competitive posturing.
However, there are times when the market simply rejects a
product or the product misses the mark. When this occurs,
hypergrowth executives keep close to customers, chart a new
course, and stay focused on their responsibilities.

Keep Close to Customers

During hypergrowth, Seagate Technology found out that 1 in
every 20 disk drives it shipped failed within three months of
installation. The crashes stemmed from contaminated media
used in its drives. As a result, Apple Computer canceled its
orders for 3 1/2-inch drives and IBM found other supply sources.

In an effort to reduce the failure rates of Seagate's hard drives
and hold on to his customers, Alan Shugart adopted critical
quality control measures. He opened repair plants at facilities
of every major distributor, then totally revamped Seagate's 3 1/2-
inch manufacturing line.

Chart a New Course

Compaq missed the market with its Telecompaq computer design. Rod Canion established a 50-employee subsidiary to develop a state-of-the-art, IBM-compatible desktop computer
whose functions included a telephone, clock, calculator, and
calendar. A vote of confidence for the product came when

telecommunications companies chose to distribute the mixed-breed machine.

Compaq, however, overlooked its prime business tenet: Understand the customer. Managers refused to pay double the personal computer price when a $500 terminal and speed dialer delivered similar Telecompaq features. Ironically, distribution also played a key role in Telecompaq's setback. Differences in phone systems made the Telecompaq hard to hook up. Equally important, the buying decision required input from both computer and telecom managers. The Telecompaq was left with no one to champion it.

Although the subsidiary closed down, the investment was still beneficial as Telecompaq technology was incorporated into other products. Compaq management clearly demonstrated its ability to pull out of a tailspin and chart a new course.

Never Lose Sight of Your Responsibilities

Fred Smith always viewed overnight delivery as a compromise for the true demand of his customers. So after five years of planning, Federal Express introduced its two-hour ZapMail facsimile document transmission service.

While averaging only 2,000 transmissions a day, ZapMail required 10 times that volume just to break even. To boost business, Smith slashed ZapMail's price and mounted an aggressive ad campaign. He also encouraged overnight mail customers to trade up to ZapMail as he increased the cost of Federal's overnight letter.

Fred Smith made two fundamental errors early on that came back to haunt him. He entered the two-hour mail delivery market uncertain of its size. He also invested in technology assuming that the office of the future would be paper-dependent. Taking advantage of these mistakes, MCI countered with its own version of electronic mail, betting that PC communications would make ZapMail obsolete. Facsimile manufacturers then attacked Federal Express with claims that owning a fax machine was more cost-effective than using ZapMail.

To fend off the competitive threats, Smith installed ZapMail machines at his customers' locations to eliminate the courier delay. Then he designed a satellite transmission network to bypass the phone companies. Smith's proposed telecommunications path mimicked his overnight hub-and-spoke distribution system as each item was beamed to Memphis for an address check, then forwarded on to its destination. Although the FCC approved his request for a satellite launch date, suddenly Smith discontinued his ZapMail service.

Quite simply, ZapMail's communications system didn't align with the market demand. Moreover, the drain on Federal Express proved excessive as the two-year ZapMail experiment closed down with a pre-tax write-off totaling $357 million. This decision demonstrated Fred Smith's concern for the best interest of his shareholders and employees. Federal Express absorbed more than 1,300 ZapMail workers into other areas of service. Mr. Smith then refocused to defend his leadership position in the overnight industry he pioneered.

Principle: The best defense is a good offense.

IF YOU LOSE YOUR BIGGEST ACCOUNT

When you provide great customer service you can expect customer loyalty in return. However, when loyal customers place unreasonable demands upon your organization, something has to give. Often it is the business relationship. Successful companies, at times, lose big accounts. The key is to cultivate the rest of your customer base so you don't place all of your proverbial eggs in one basket. Here's a good rule of thumb: Don't lose your biggest account unless you can maintain profitability and a positive cash flow from the balance of your customer base.

Avoid the "All or Nothing" Tactic

As the personal computer industry's sales dropped from its 90 percent annual hypergrowth rate to a more sedate 20 percent clip, Businessland looked for ways to up its margins. David

Norman started by squeezing a 44 percent discount out of IBM. He then asked Compaq to match that figure.

Rod Canion was leery of this request since Businessland had been nudging ever closer to the IBM camp. Compaq knew that IBM's market development funds, earmarked for advertising and sales training, were supplementing Businessland commissions for sales of IBM products. When David Norman voted for IBM's Micro Channel architecture as the PC standard, this left the Compaq-led Extended Industry Standard Architecture out in the cold.

Instead of complying with Norman's request, Canion abruptly revoked Businessland's reseller agreement. Clearly hurt by the spat, Norman tried to make up the $150 million in lost Compaq sales by promoting NeXT, NCR, and NetFrame computers. Businessland's subsequent shortfall resulted in a series of quarterly losses and personnel layoffs.

Weigh Major Decisions Carefully

Compaq decided to go without Businessland's distribution channel. While Compaq product sales accounted for 15 percent of Businessland's revenues, Compaq earned just 7 percent of its income from Businessland distribution. Rod Canion felt that brand recognition and price performance would carry Compaq sales.

David Norman claimed that Compaq had walked away from the premier channel to the corporate market. Canion, on the other hand, argued that corporate buyers were not loyal to vendors, but migrated to the best value in technology. Compaq counted on loyal customers buying its products through other distribution channels. However, Compaq misjudged the market. Cooling PC sales combined with weak distribution caused Compaq's first earnings drop in its short history.

Put Egos Aside and Get Back to Business

After a 13-month separation, Businessland and Compaq found out that they needed each other. As part of their reconciliation,

Businessland accepted Compaq's standard discount and geared up to once again sell Compaq products. Compaq also forced Enzo Torresi to resign from Businessland's Board of Directors. Torresi was a Businessland executive who had encouraged David Norman to emphasize IBM product sales over the other brands. During Businessland's 13-month hiatus with Compaq, Torresi went on to become CEO of NetFrame, a Compaq competitor.

Principle: Greedy pigs go to slaughter.

IF YOUR EARNINGS COLLAPSE

Publicly traded companies are required to summarize the income earned by each holder of company stock. A popular ratio used is the earnings per share, which simply divides the company's earnings by the common shares of stock outstanding. A collapse in earnings is often caused by the costs associated with financing rapid expansion. To bolster earnings, hypergrowth executives focus on the basics, trim the fat, then regain profitability.

Focus on Business Basics

Leslie Wexner was convinced that imported clothes would someday influence American design. To prepare for hypergrowth, he visited Europe on a monthly basis. Then he acquired factories in the Orient to produce original merchandise for sale at half the price of fashion trend leaders.

Leslie Wexner took The Limited public after opening his sixth store. He then borrowed heavily to acquire other stores. After his retail empire reached 360 stores, Wexner got into financial trouble. Overexpansion caused his corporate earnings to collapse.

A chastened Wexner relinquished control of store administration to his vice chairman, Bob Morosky. Wexner, however, never lost sight of his mission. He simply focused on a basic business formula that would lead his company into hyper-growth: efficient manufacturing and the rapid distribution of trendy fashion knock-offs.

Trim the Fat

After MCI was granted the right to compete in the long distance phone business, rates dropped by 30 percent. This caused MCI to lose most of its price advantage over AT&T and exerted extreme pressure on MCI's margins.

MCI laid off 16 percent of its workforce to consolidate operations. Most of the layoffs occurred in its top-heavy tele-marketing and marketing divisions, which implemented the "equal-access" drive for choosing a long-distance carrier.

Several MCI facilities were then closed to eliminate duplication. These moves trimmed $100 million in operating costs, $50 million from annual depreciation, and more than $100 million from capital expenditures. MCI took nearly a $700 million pre-tax charge against earnings that reflected the reduced value of old satellite equipment plus severance pay and consolidation costs.

To recover from its millions in losses, MCI focused on becoming a high-value service provider. They increased penetration into new markets such as toll-free calling and international phone service and won corporate customers away from AT&T. The year after its layoffs, MCI posted an $88 million profit. More importantly, traffic on its network grew by 25 percent—twice the rate of growth for the industry as a whole.

Regain Profitability

Bernard Marcus became the star of do-it-yourself marketing when Home Depot's stock reached 31¾ . . . 77 times its earnings. Convinced his concept could work anywhere, Marcus doubled the number of Home Depot stores in less than a year.

However, his rapid expansion encompassed several new markets. To fuel this growth, Marcus borrowed $200 million for inventory, advertising, and personnel. Home Depot's advertising costs tripled and its promotional pricing cut into earnings. Management's attention then got diverted to stores where sales lagged.

Marcus had opened so many new stores that expansion outpaced his supply of qualified staff. The need to fill in shifts at new stores caused sales training to get passed over. Even worse, inventory management unraveled as some stores begged for merchandise while others received unneeded goods.

Finally, Home Depot's success formula broke down when Marcus paid $38.4 million (163 percent over book value) for the 9-store Bowater chain. Not only was Bowater's reputation and morale at an all-time low, its inventory did not match Home Depot's. As a result, Home Depot's net earnings declined by 42 percent from record levels the previous year. For the first time, Wall Street's faith in Home Depot wavered as its stock prices collapsed.

Marcus quickly responded by putting a tough new operations plan in place. He sold Home Depot's four Detroit stores, upped margins to regain profitability, trimmed the expansion schedule by half and worked sedulously to turn around the Bowater chain.

Marcus then strengthened Home Depot's corporate infrastructure by hiring top-notch management personnel, including a director of training, and vice presidents of operations and merchandising. With the help of a new stock offering, Marcus reduced his debt and financed Home Depot's computerized inventory control system. Finally, Marcus chose to expand within his existing markets. This fill-in saturation strategy became an efficient and profitable path to growth.

Principle: Getting big won't matter unless you're profitable.

IF YOU GET SUED

One of the most frustrating experiences in business is getting slapped with a lawsuit. While the natural instinct is to establish a defense and fight, over time lawsuits become a financial drain. They not only retard a company's growth as new business opportunities go unnoticed, lawsuits can also send a company into an emotional tailspin. When they get sued, hypergrowth executives tend to either settle quickly or fight to the end.

Settle Lawsuits Quickly

Liz Claiborne was open to all new opportunities for growth. She not only diversified into various licensing agreements, Claiborne embarked on a joint venture with Avon Products, Inc. It was here that Claiborne lost control of what she did best.

Liz Claiborne saw a great opportunity to link with a worldwide manufacturer of cosmetic fragrances. She brought retail marketing expertise to the partnership while Avon provided global manufacturing resources. Together they produced a line of Liz Claiborne fragrances and cosmetics for the workday.

The fragrance, however, lacked the hype necessary for success as only $5 million was spent to promote the product—just one-third the budget of its hot-selling competitor Obsession. Claiborne also refused to provide gifts with purchases, a common industry promotional technique. The partnership ran into more problems when Avon entered into a conflicting joint venture that constituted a breach in their agreement. Arguments led to lawsuits and the relationship was quickly dissolved.

Fight to the End

Tele-Communications, Inc. had become known as the cable industry's toughest competitor. John Malone once sued the city of Boulder, Colorado, over TCI's right to wire the entire city for cable. The case went to the U.S. Supreme Court and TCI won. However, TCI found a different verdict when it was sued by Jefferson City, the capitol of Missouri.

Five years after TCI began managing the cable system in Jefferson City, it won a three-year franchise extension. Just before that contract was to expire, the city council issued a request for proposals. The invitation to bid resulted from TCI's slow response to improve its cable service. When TCI refused to participate in the bidding, the city council awarded the franchise to a local group of businessmen. The mayor of Jefferson City then reversed the council's decision and gave the cable rights back to TCI.

The local group filed suit charging that TCI had illegally conspired with the mayor to retain the franchise in violation of antitrust laws. TCI argued that its actions were protected by the First Amendment's right to petition government. Malone then countered with a lawsuit and threated to cut off service, sell inexpensive satellite dishes plus undermine any cable company that took TCI's place.

Once the case reached the Supreme Court, TCI further argued that the city had no right to award an exclusive franchise to another system. The Justices didn't buy Malone's arguments and responded to TCI's First Amendment pleas by declaring that the Constitution prevents such winner-take-all politics for the right of expression through the cable medium. TCI lost the case as the ruling narrowed its First Amendment protections.

When damages were assessed, the local competitor was given its choice of $32.4 million (triple damages for violating the Sherman Antitrust Act) or $35.8 million for violations of Missouri State law. TCI's final bill totaled more than $43 million in damages and interest for a broadcast area servicing only 35,000 residents.

The expensive and embarrasing decision against Malone marked the first time a city constituted a "natural monopoly" for cable television. The ruling also dictated that cities have a right to get the best service for its citizens at the best price. TCI's decision to fight to the end opened the door for government re-regulation of the volatile cable industry.

Principle: A lawsuit means the party's over.

WHEN YOUR COMPETITORS WISE UP

When you're successful, competitors emerge from all directions. John Malone and TCI, for example, experienced intense competitive pressures from outside the cable industry. Movie

moguls lobbied for cable re-regulation while telephone companies cried for cable access through the lifting of federal restrictions. New technologies, such as direct satellite broadcasting,
also threatened Malone's hold on the industry as programmers
tried to bypass TCI altogether.

Success also found The Price Club competing with many
forms of retailing as it married retail and wholesale to food and
nonfood merchandising. Its high volume business challenged
so many rules of retailing that competitors wondered whether
it was a store, a warehouse, a market, or a distribution channel.
The Price Club's competitors came to include other warehouse clubs, wholesale distributors, supermarkets, and catalog
stores.

Warehouse Club Competition

The Price Club's warehouses typically display an operating area
of 100,000 square feet with 25-foot-high ceilings. Open seven
days a week, they carry 4,000 different stock keeping units
valued at $4 million. This inventory turns about 16 times a
year—five times faster than a Kmart, but one-third slower than a
supermarket. With labor costs amounting to 5 percent of sales
and operating margins hovering around 10 percent, the entry
barrier was so high that it actually took six years for The Price
Club to attract its first direct competition:

- *Pace Membership Warehouse* became the first club competitor when its Denver, Colorado, warehouse opened.
  Pace operates under The Price Club formula, yet its integrated computer system ties daily sales into accounting.
  This gives Pace control over inventory items that turn every
  few days.

- *Sam's Wholesale Club* began when Sam Walton, chairman
  of Wal-Mart, took over a former GEX store in Oklahoma
  City, Oklahoma. Walton shifted away from occupying
  abandoned retail sites to constructing his own custom
  warehouses. With its higher ceiling design, Sam's can ac-
  commodate even more merchandise on its selling floor.

- *Costco Wholesale Club* opened its first store in Seattle, Washington. It was founded by two entrepreneurs, one a former Price Club vice president. Costco most closely resembles The Price Club operation by maintaining the same wholesale and retail sales balance.

- *The Wholesale Club* opened its first store in Indianapolis, Indiana. Located near blue-collar pockets and operating at a 10 percent margin, the Wholesale Club did not follow The Price Club's lead of charging group members an annual fee.

- *The Warehouse Club* was founded by the former vice chairman of Kmart who worked for The Price Club long enough to learn its formula. Started in Niles, Illinois, it resembled traditional retailing more than warehouse wholesaling. However, its close ties to manufacturers resulted in product packaging design breakthroughs.

- *B.J.'s Wholesale Club* opened in Providence, Rhode Island, as a Zayre's spinoff. B.J.'s buyers, however, remained autonomous from Zayre's merchandisers. Although B.J.'s targets populations of 500,000 or more, they forego expensive retail sites.

- *Makro,* based in Cincinnati, Ohio, caters only to wholesale customers. With warehouses measuring twice the size of a typical Price Club, Makro locates in areas with at least 75,000 potential business customers. This is four times the number of prospects required to support The Price Club which accepts nonwholesale groups.

Wholesaler/Distributor Competition

The Price Club became a threat to wholesalers when it penetrated the independent retailers and food service companies. The highly fragmented wholesaler-distributor, with inadequate efficiencies, took the biggest blow from The Price Club presence. Trying to compete on a price basis devastated their gross profit margins.

For protection, distributors looked to minimum pricing laws. The entrenched distributors were ultimately forced to improve service to fend off The Price Club threat. Wholesalers who won back lost customers did so through value-added service offerings.

Supermarket Competition

Since food represents 26 percent of The Price Club sales, supermarkets were concerned by its presence. This forced supermarkets to reduce prices and compete on a cost basis.

Supermarkets in small towns were not affected by the warehouse revolution, since Price Clubs require larger population densities to support its stores. However, as new clubs entered the market, the need to attract customers intensified. New competitors began deviating from The Price Club formula by offering more food varieties and stocking smaller sizes. While this drew more customers away from the supermarket's customer base, it also crushed their margins.

Catalog Competition

The Price Club also took sales from the catalog showroom industry. Catalog showrooms, however, held their own in jewelry and fit sales. These categories didn't turn fast enough for The Price Club formula and required special buying expertise.

The catalog showroom's strength was no longer offering the lowest price in town. Although Price Clubs often beat a catalog showroom's price on a specific item, they rarely stocked the same merchandise from week to week. Catalogers exploited this weakness by repositioning their business based on stability of supply.

Defend Against the Competition

The Price Club, in each case, defended the territory it captured from competitors. Against warehouse clubs, its hypergrowth was fueled due to a superior understanding of wholesale merchandise content, pre-opening solicitation procedures, bulk merchandise handling, plus food and general merchandise buying disciplines. The Price Club also defended its pricing tactics with wholesalers and distributors through heavy product rebating. It became classified as an entity outside the traditional wholesale and retail boundaries. After The Price Club lured shoppers into spending more of their grocery budgets away from traditional supermarkets, they then increased consumer appeal by adding more perishables to their inventories. With catalog competition, The Price Club simply focused on offering the lowest prices on appliances and photography, which became the major catalog showroom casualties.

Competitive Sins

While attacking your market and defending yourself against your competition, beware of the following eight competitive sins. These represent the most common mistakes made by companies on the road to hypergrowth:

- *Sin 1: Dilute product assortment.* Once a product starts selling well, a natural move is to broaden the assortment. While sustaining consumer interest is important, the key is to introduce only those products that accelerate inventory turnover.

- *Sin 2: Grow without profits.* With success comes the desire to expand quickly. However, winning market share without turning a profit is a shortcut to early retirement.

- *Sin 3: Wander from the hypergrowth formula.* As competition emerges, a growing company can lose sight of the basics. Fending off competitive threats can cause leaders to forget why they succeeded in the first place.

- *Sin 4: Relax cost controls.* In a competitive market, the company with the lowest cost structure wins. Hypergrowth momentum is maintained by keeping a tight grip on pricing disciplines.

- *Sin 5: Enter saturated markets.* Access to a large cross-section of customers is an important hypergrowth component. However, paying too much money to enter crowded markets leads to a loss of productivity per square foot.

- *Sin 6: Ignore your customers.* Although expenses and administrative costs must stay low, employees are still the ones who deliver service to your customers. Happy employees are productive and experience low turnover rates.

- *Sin 7: Lose control over logistics.* Hypergrowth cannot occur with seat-of-the-pants management. Success requires total control over ordering, invoicing, receiving, stocking, pricing, and shrinkage.

- *Sin 8: Forego training.* Only trained personnel can sustain hypergrowth momentum. Expanding beyond the supply of knowledgable staff has doomed many a company on the path to hypergrowth.

Principle: In business, you either make dust or you eat dust.

IF YOUR LEGISLATORS WREAK HAVOC

The most powerful force in America is the legislative body of Congress. It can displace entire industries with the slam of a gavel. Federal legislators, who pass nearly 200 new laws each year, often catch unsuspecting companies in the line of fire. When market forces clash with legislative power, a backlash can wreak havoc in the marketplace. To cope with the impact of emerging laws, companies analyze their options then adjust quickly when new legislation is passed.

Prepare for Legislation

Liz Claiborne, Reebok, The Limited, and other manufacturers who depend on foreign manufacturing sources faced ominous problems as protectionist sentiment, a falling dollar, and trade restrictions became the warning signs of pending legislation.

The Limited prepared for potential legislation by acquiring Mast Industries. As Leslie Wexner's buying arm, Mast formed joint ventures with foreign manufacturers in locations free of U.S. apparel import restrictions. Liz Claiborne management responded to the protectionist trend by fostering industrial development at home. They helped a Hong Kong manufacturer establish a modern stitching facility in New York City.

Protectionist legislation also spurred the Reebok staff to check out new manufacturing sites in China, Indonesia, and Mexico. Developing alternate sources of supply let Paul Fireman expand Reebok's production capacity and improve its quality control.

Adjust Quickly to New Laws

Business came rolling in for Integrated Resources when a new law made real estate shelters an attractive investment vehicle. Just three years later, Congress removed many of those benefits and put a halt to contrived tax losses that shielded ordinary personal income. Finally, a legislative assault known as Tax Reform ripped apart tax shelters and wreaked havoc on Integrated Resources's investment portfolio. On the day Senator Robert Packwood's (R-Oregon) Tax Reform Plan was announced, it not only deprived investors of some $50 billion in shelters, it caused Integrated's stock to experience the biggest percentage loss on the New York Stock Exchange.

Since Integrated Resources was the master builder of deep tax shelters for its wealthy investors, Selig Zises fought hard to preserve his business base. He prophesied that Packwood's Plan would drive up the price of exisiting buildings and decimate new construction. Once Tax Reform passed, Zises watched his company's earnings decline, demand for new shelters plummet, and investors disappear.

To survive, Integrated Resources spent the next two years changing the entire spectrum of its business. Zises raised up a salesforce of former stock brokers and created the nation's sixth-largest securities firm based on registered representatives. He then launched television ad campaigns pitching

Integrated's expanded line of products and services. To finance these moves, Zises raised hundreds of millions of dollars through junk bond dealers. This fund-raising effort eventually quintupled Integrated's long-term debt to $1.9 billion.

As Integrated Resources branched out from its elitist roots, its survival was tied to reaching middle income investors who needed life insurance and investment advisory services. In place of deep tax shelters, Zises offered a new generation of public real estate partnerships that were long on cash profits and short on write-offs.

Less than two years after legislation was inacted, Integrated's total sales grew 41 percent to $1.1 billion and its stock value nearly doubled. Zises tried to spur additional demand for real estate partnerships through income-oriented investments without tax benefits. Yet, the burden of deepening debt and the lack of investors to finance its negative cash flow buried Integrated Resources. Selig Zises resigned just prior to his company defaulting on $955 million of short-term debt.

Principle: If you live by the sword, you'll die by it too.

IF FATIGUE SETS IN

Leading a company into hypergrowth is not a 9-to-5 job. At stretches it demands 18-hour days. Two problems fast growth executives face are fatigue and illness. To combat these demons, take extended vacations, bring in experienced replacements, or simply retire from the business altogether.

Take a Leave of Absence

The fact that Sam Walton founded Wal-Mart long triggered speculation of who could succeed him. At one point, Walton resigned as chairman and chief executive officer, but he returned two years later to resume charge of his company. He again took a leave of absence to show Wall Street that Wal-Mart could run without him. However, he got antsy and returned to work after just four months off.

Although Walton's bout with leukemia forced him to relinquish day-to-day control of his stores, he remained the one in charge. His potential successors found this out when he made the chief financial officer and chief operating officer actually switch jobs.

When Walton's leukemia went into remission, he spearheaded the phenomenal diversification effort of his retail empire. This included Sam's Wholesale Clubs, Helen's Arts and Crafts stores, **dot** Discount Drug stores, and Hypermart*U.S.A.

Bring in Experienced Replacements

While taking MCI into hypergrowth, Bill McGowan worked 16-hour days, ate poorly, smoked incessantly, and experienced heart problems. Close to death at age 59, McGowan became the first chief executive officer of a Fortune 500 company to successfully undergo a heart transplant.

Following the operation, McGowan spent five weeks in the hospital. He returned to his home and waited another six weeks before returning to work. After less than a day at the office, McGowan retreated to his beach house for another month of rest. There McGowan changed his habits. He ate better, quit smoking, and committed to work just ten-hour days with weekends off.

During his recovery, McGowan turned the reigns over to MCI president Bert Roberts and brought Orville Wright, former president and vice chairman, out of retirement. They immediately convened 22 of the company's top executives to look for answers to some tough questions: "Can we survive this?," "Will the regulatory situation turn around?," "Are we in the right business?"

The consensus among the leaders was to stay in the long distance business, tighten their belts, focus on big customers and develop new services. Soon after, McGowan and MCI both returned to full health.

Enjoy What You've Achieved

After 39 years in the fashion design industry, 13 years running her own company, and a decade of hypergrowth, Liz Claiborne retired from active management in the company she founded. Claiborne, who turned 60, stated that both she and her husband, Arthur, would remain on as directors of the company. Their initial plans were to pursue a number of environmental, social, and personal interests.

Several years were spent preparing their eventual successors. Liz and Arthur played consultant and teacher during the last couple of years of the company's hypergrowth. Liz raised up a team of designers and Arthur trained new administrators. The future direction was to continue down the same path they had established.

They announced that co-founder, Jerome Chazen, would take over as chairman. Chief financial officer, Harvey Falk, then moved up to vice chairman and president. The management successors, however, inherited some big challenges. After Liz Claiborne busted through the billion-dollar barrier, earnings were hurt by a slowdown in consumer spending. The new management team then discovered that expansion into retail, with its First Issue stores, became a financial burden.

Nonetheless, Liz Claiborne had left her mark on the fashion world. She passed up the glamour of evening wear to design clothing for millions of professional women who had re-entered the workforce. Market research even showed that American women viewed Liz Claiborne as a personal friend, one whose tastes and judgement they trusted.

Liz Claiborne and Arthur Ortenberg bowed out with a short press statement, "Our decision to retire is at root a very simple one. After years of working long, long days, and then meeting the new challenges of helping to grow and manage a billion-dollar enterprise, we are looking forward to making time to devote to personal interests and to enjoying the fruits of our labor."

Principle: When you go, go out on top!

HOW TO PREPARE FOR THE UNEXPECTED

While most people simply react to unexpected events, hyper-growth leaders learn to anticipate them. Unexpected events represent a barrier to hypergrowth on the one hand, yet can reveal new growth opportunities on the other. The following three-pronged approach can help you prepare for the unexpected:

1. Establish a Point of Reference

Hypergrowth is a global phenomenon with real-time demands. Information from the following seven categories reflects such activities and serves as hypergrowth's point of reference:

- *New products.* New products and patented processes are major sources of unexpected activity that can render your current offering obsolete or uncover a hypergrowth opportunity.
- *Competitive moves.* Your competition is in business to increase sales, increase profits, and increase market share— and if you're not monitoring their moves, it will be at your expense.
- *New legislation.* While federal legislation often sinks unsuspecting companies, state and local politicians can also provide hypergrowth openings for perceptive executives.
- *Industry shifts.* It is not unusual for an entire industry to change direction in response to shifts in the costs of energy, capital, or labor.
- *Market patterns.* The purchasing habits of specific market segments can provide valuable insights into places where new events may unfold.
- *Mergers and acquisitions.* Leveraged buyouts and corporate acquisitions often provide the needed resources to fuel the hypergrowth process.
- *Global growth.* Although new markets can emerge as quickly as established ones close down, the risks of doing

business in foreign countries is counter-balanced by the potential for big returns.

2. Establish an Information Network

The best way to prepare for unexpected events is to stay informed. These 40 inexpensive and readily available sources of information will help you turn unexpected events into hypergrowth opportunities:

- *Advertisements* provide insights into competitive products such as positioning, features, benefits, costs, and targeted markets.
- *Advocacy groups* provide a great source of new activity since they are organized catalysts of change.
- *Agents* and the entire spectrum of middleman wholesale distributors can tell you why products sell and which new product launches will succeed.
- *Annual reports* provide a biased company overview, yet are free just by calling the company's investor relations department.
- *Associations* host meetings and publish materials that provide valuable insights into industry, market, and competitive activities.
- *Attorneys* are a good source of market information as they represent important business and financial concerns.
- *Bibliographic references* are entire books of compiled reports, surveys, market information, and industry data available through local university business school libraries.
- *Bureau of Labor* provides stacks of statistics including productivity data for different regions of the country.
- *Clipping services* are a great way to extract specific company news or general topic updates from thousands of current periodicals and newspapers.
- *Competitors* are a great resource since they share common challenges in the marketplace.

- *Company publications* including press releases, newsletters, and educational resources provide valuable insights into competitive offerings.

- *Consultants* who have extensive knowledge of business niches can provide important data about emerging markets.

- *Court records* of federal and state court trial testimony can reveal sensitive information about companies.

- *Credit agencies* sell detailed credit information about businesses just like yours.

- *Customers* provide tremendous feedback regarding market needs, new products, distribution channels, services, quality problems, competitor strengths and weaknesses, and much more.

- *Databases* offer real-time data about companies, industries, business news, finances, patents and trademarks, biographies, demographics, forecasts, public disclosures, foreign countries, and more.

- *Directories,* available in local libraries, offer detailed listings of companies by size, industry, and geography that can translate into market, supplier, customer, and competitor intelligence.

- *Federal government* (through the Superintendent of Documents in Washington, DC) offers a broad range of statistics and market studies from its 27 major regulatory agencies.

- *FDIC* publishes reports and newsletters that monitor trends and government affairs impacting the financial community.

- *Freedom of Information Act* requires the U.S. government to release documents in government files to anyone requesting them.

- *Help-wanted ads* provide insights into competitive activities by revealing expansion plans, R&D programs, production problems, and key personnel changes.

- *Infopreneurs* are independent information specialists who gather, organize, and disseminate information about any problem that needs solving.

- *Journalists* are information gathering machines who will exchange their insights for news story leads.
- *Library of Congress* carries an extensive collection of books, periodicals, and information ranging from government-sponsored researchers to Third World exporters.
- *Local governments* provide business and economic updates on a local level through the Chamber of Commerce, Economic Development Office, Labor Office, Tax Assessor, Building Department, or County Clerk.
- *Local newspapers* report news rarely picked up by wire services such as hirings, firings, new contracts, management changes, plant expansions, and closings.
- *Market research firms* provide industry-specific market studies, product viability reports, promotional analyses, and surveys about market conditions.
- *Patent and Trademark Office* provides information on every new registration through its publications and abstracts.
- *Periodicals* which cover the general, business, and financial marketplaces are great sources of information about the business climate.
- *Reference reports,* available in research libraries, provide specific information on trade, finances, raw materials, production capacities, government regulations, technology trends, economic climate, plus a myriad of other topics.
- *Reverse engineering* is accomplished by technicians who tear apart competing products to examine the materials, specifications, production techniques, components, and technologies used to design and build them.
- *Security analyst reports* are valuable when monitoring competition and projecting future performance.
- *Securities and Exchange Commission* provides detailed financial information about public companies on a quarterly and annual basis through 10-Q and 10-K reports.
- *Speeches* delivered by executives and industry experts often reveal interesting facts that can be found in a library's periodical section under the title *Vital Speeches of the Day.*

- *State government agencies* have on file articles of incorporation, actions taken against companies by regulatory agencies, consumer complaints involving products and services, financial information on companies that have borrowed against their assets, and lots more.

- *Stockbrokers* have access to detailed research on companies and industries from an investment standpoint.

- *Suppliers* have more hands-on data about market conditions, new products, and competitive information than any other resource.

- *Trade publications* provide great data on industry trends, market statistics, executive profiles, and competitive analyses.

- *Trade shows* provide a rich source of information on new products through exhibitor literature and personal contact.

- *Unions* can leak information about companies during negotiations such as wages, contract terms, productivity rates, automation plans, and more.

3. Establish an Early Warning System

Learning to expect the unexpected requires access to vast information resources, skills for handling the raw data, and a person who will take responsibility for processing the data into useful knowledge. The first step is to subscribe to the best sources of information. Then, organize your system to collect only the relevant data. Next, establish a distribution network so that key decision makers can receive relevant and timely information. Finally, plan for periodic strategic reviews to answer the following questions, which address the common sources of unexpected events:

1. What aspects about your company are unique?
2. How will your business change over the next five years?
3. What do your customers consider the most valued feature of your products?

4. Which major customers are least satisfied with your offerings?

5. Which customers do you sell to that your biggest competitors don't?

6. How are your customers' needs likely to change over the next five years?

7. What are three potential substitutes for your product?

8. Why do your customers use your product instead of the substitutes?

9. What would it take for these substitutes to become a competitive threat to your company?

10. In what ways is your company vulnerable to competitive threats?

11. What are the real differences between your products and those of your competitors?

12. What strategies do your competitors implement to stimulate customer loyalty and repeat business?

13. What is the most effective distribution channel in your industry?

14. How much could you cut margins before losing profitability?

15. How much capital can you access in short notice to survive a pricing war or a recession?

16. How can you improve access to your market, suppliers, and labor pool?

17. How would you rate your management's depth and skill level relative to your competition?

18. How can your company structure be altered to quickly enter emerging markets?

19. What aspects of government intervention pose the greatest threats to your business strategy?

20. What foreign suppliers currently compete with your offerings?

Getting organized to expect the unexpected requires exposure to the right sources of information. Rechannel these oceans of data into streams of strategic intelligence. While information technology provides the advantages of speed and analytical power, trained personnel are still needed to assess this intelligence in light of your company's performance and goals. Using this strategy to identify unexpected events in the marketplace will improve your odds of entering into hypergrowth.

III

Hypergrowth
Hall of Fame

The Hypergrowth
Hall of Fame

The Hypergrowth Hall of Fame consists of companies that emerged from start-up, relative dormancy, or standard growth into hypergrowth that was sustained for a decade under the same economic conditions. As you contemplate their accomplishments, consider how they did it:

EDUCATION COMES FROM THE MARKETPLACE, NOT THE CLASSROOM

- Liz Claiborne never graduated from high school; Steve Jobs and Paul Fireman both had enough of college after just one semester. So where did they learn how to build their billion-dollar companies? From the marketplace.
- Pharmacy school didn't teach Bernard Marcus about specialty retailing, nor did a degree in physics teach Alan Shugart how to design disk drives for a global market.
- John Malone's Ph.D. didn't land him a job in the cable industry, and Rod Canion's Ph.D. (minus dissertation) didn't show him how to start a computer company 13 years after leaving school.

- Fred Smith wasn't satisfied with the 'C' that Yale's Professor Challis Hall gave him on the economics paper that described his hub-and-spoke express delivery service. He just went out and did it!

- Even Sam Walton's business degree was obsolete by the time the discount industry emerged twenty years after his graduation.

So what good is school?

School is where you learn how to learn, learn how to choose, and learn how to relate. Earning a college degree shows an employer that you can achieve a long-term goal. School can even impart specific knowledge that may save you time and money when starting out. But, no college degree ever started a company or achieved hypergrowth.

PUT THE NEEDS OF CUSTOMERS AHEAD OF YOUR OWN DESIRES

You'll get what you want from life only after you've given enough other people what they want. The market shows us each day what it wants . . . and these 15 executives really gave it what it wanted. Their annual compensation packages averaged $1.9 million. The value of stock held by these hypergrowth executives ranged from $6.1 million to $4.5 billion. Removing Sam Walton's billions to avoid skewing, the average amount of stock owned by the other 14 hypergrowth executives was $146 million. By the way, their combined net worth is three times the value of all the tea in China, which totals $1.8 billion.

YOU ARE NEVER TOO YOUNG OR TOO OLD TO MEET MARKET NEEDS

Hypergrowth starts with identifying a need in the market followed up with a product or a service that meets that need. Finding a hypergrowth opportunity can come at any time or any age. These executives embarked on their hypergrowth ventures at ages ranging from 21 to 49:

21	Steve Jobs/Apple Computer
23	Leslie Wexner/The Limited
26	Fred Smith/Federal Express
26	Selig Zises/Integrated Resources
31	Charles Wang/Computer Associates
32	John Malone/TCI
33	Robert Price/The Price Club
35	Paul Fireman/Reebok
37	Rod Canion/Compaq
40	Bill McGowan/MCI
45	David Norman/Businessland
46	Sam Walton/Wal-Mart
47	Elisabeth Claiborne Ortenberg/Liz Claiborne
48	Alan Shugart/Seagate Technology
49	Bernard Marcus/Home Depot

WITH HYPERGROWTH YOU BECOME ACCOUNTABLE

Each hypergrowth company became publicly traded shortly after start-up. Most trade on the New York Stock Exchange except for Apple, The Price Club, MCI, TCI, and Seagate, which are found on the NASDAQ Exchange. The Limited, Compaq, and Wal-Mart all trade on multiple exchanges.

While the American dream is to come directly out of the gates and enter into hypergrowth, very few companies ever achieve it. In most cases there are growth spurts, set backs, then adjustments until hypergrowth kicks in. The average number of years a company had been in business prior to the start of hypergrowth was six.

While going public may be considered a rite of passage in business, your life and your company suddenly become an open book. You are required to reveal your business secrets to the entire world. Everyone knows that your brother-in-law is on the payroll, along with all the details of your compensation package. This is known as accountability.

As a public company, your focus shifts from long-term growth and profits to short-term earnings. Once you go public, you are not just accountable to the marketplace. You've also got investors breathing down your neck.

BLOOM WHERE YOU ARE PLANTED

New York is famous for its garment district (Liz Claiborne) and as the financial capitol of the world (Integrated Resources). Silicon Valley is known as the high-tech capital of the world (Apple, Businessland, Seagate). So then why does America's fastest hypergrowth start-up (Compaq) emerge from Houston? And why does Sam Walton (Wal-Mart) become a multi-billionaire from Bentonville, Arkansas, population 10,000? And how can a guy like Paul Fireman go broke twice from Canton, Massachusetts, then emerge with a billion-dollar athletic shoe company (Reebok) without leaving town? The answer to these questions is that they all knew what they did best and stuck around to do it.

HYPERGROWTH BUILDING BLOCKS

Now that you've examined all facets of hypergrowth, now that you've been inspired by those who've achieved it, remember, to achieve hypergrowth, start with the basics.

Building Block 1: Develop Amazing Products & Fantastic Services

The first building block of hypergrowth requires products that are unparalleled in quality and supported by superior service. Encourage your technical people to swap information that improves product durability and utility. Give your research team all the resources they need to uncover the market needs. Then, take a macro view of your role and try to figure out just what business you are in. Remember, to achieve hypergrowth, you don't have to be in a superstar industry; you just have to be the superstar of *your* industry.

Building Block 2: Attract World-Class Talent

Hypergrowth requires world class efforts from ordinary people. You'll need to attract dedicated employees with great minds and big hearts. Your job as chief talent scout will be to recruit those who can get excited about your mission. Building a quality management team is vital to shaping your hypergrowth venture. Heighten each employee's sense of esteem by letting them feel like the entrepreneur running their part of the hypergrowth venture.

Building Block 3: Provide Financial Value

Finally, hypergrowth will require you to effectively allocate capital resources so you can maximize shareholder returns. Consider how to improve value and provide financial stability. Think in terms of economic value-added opportunities that produce after-tax profits. This will give shareholders exactly what they want . . . top returns.

CONCLUDING THOUGHT

If you have the vision, the drive, and the tenacity, and you focus on these fundamentals with the faith that moves mountains, you will control your destiny. Finally, when your company increases sales, improves profits, gains market share, and expands into the global marketplace, you're in hypergrowth! Congratulations.

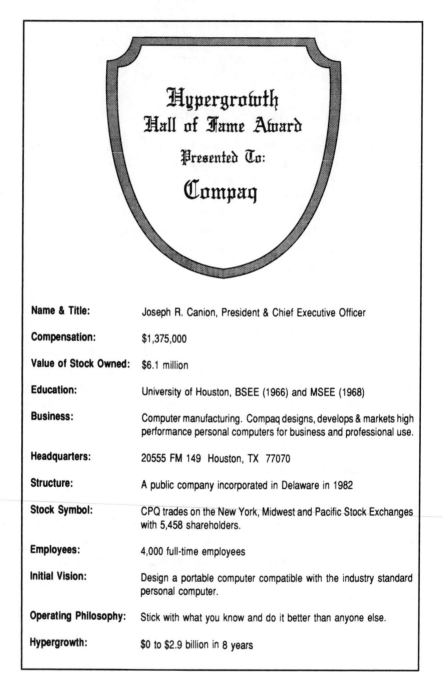

𝕳𝖞𝖕𝖊𝖗𝖌𝖗𝖔𝖜𝖙𝖍
𝕳𝖆𝖑𝖑 𝖔𝖋 𝕱𝖆𝖒𝖊 𝕬𝖜𝖆𝖗𝖉

𝕻𝖗𝖊𝖘𝖊𝖓𝖙𝖊𝖉 𝕿𝖔:

𝕮𝖔𝖒𝖕𝖆𝖖

Name & Title: Joseph R. Canion, President & Chief Executive Officer

Compensation: $1,375,000

Value of Stock Owned: $6.1 million

Education: University of Houston, BSEE (1966) and MSEE (1968)

Business: Computer manufacturing. Compaq designs, develops & markets high
                        performance personal computers for business and professional use.

Headquarters: 20555 FM 149 Houston, TX 77070

Structure: A public company incorporated in Delaware in 1982

Stock Symbol: CPQ trades on the New York, Midwest and Pacific Stock Exchanges
                        with 5,458 shareholders.

Employees: 4,000 full-time employees

Initial Vision: Design a portable computer compatible with the industry standard
                        personal computer.

Operating Philosophy: Stick with what you know and do it better than anyone else.

Hypergrowth: $0 to $2.9 billion in 8 years

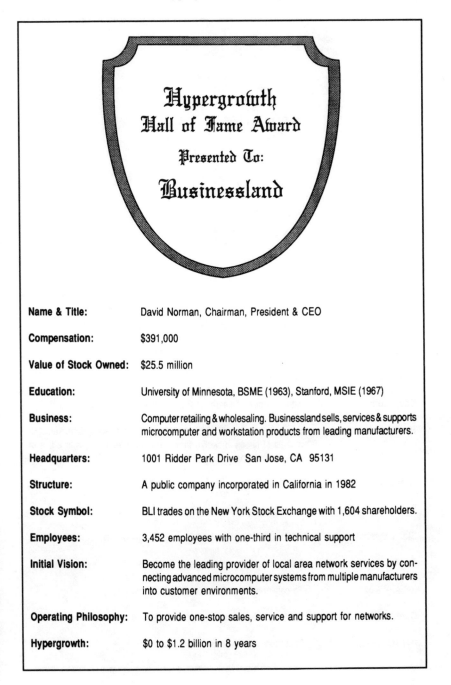

**Hypergrowth
Hall of Fame Award
Presented To:
Businessland**

Name & Title:	David Norman, Chairman, President & CEO
Compensation:	$391,000
Value of Stock Owned:	$25.5 million
Education:	University of Minnesota, BSME (1963), Stanford, MSIE (1967)
Business:	Computer retailing & wholesaling. Businessland sells, services & supports microcomputer and workstation products from leading manufacturers.
Headquarters:	1001 Ridder Park Drive San Jose, CA 95131
Structure:	A public company incorporated in California in 1982
Stock Symbol:	BLI trades on the New York Stock Exchange with 1,604 shareholders.
Employees:	3,452 employees with one-third in technical support
Initial Vision:	Become the leading provider of local area network services by connecting advanced microcomputer systems from multiple manufacturers into customer environments.
Operating Philosophy:	To provide one-stop sales, service and support for networks.
Hypergrowth:	$0 to $1.2 billion in 8 years

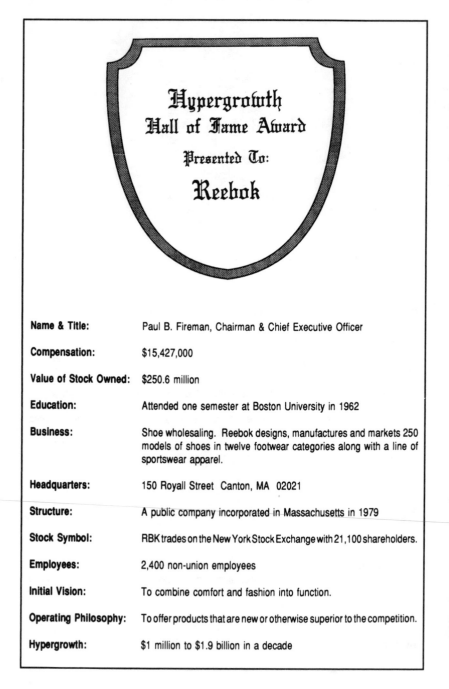

**Hypergrowth
Hall of Fame Award
Presented To:
Reebok**

Name & Title: Paul B. Fireman, Chairman & Chief Executive Officer

Compensation: $15,427,000

Value of Stock Owned: $250.6 million

Education: Attended one semester at Boston University in 1962

Business: Shoe wholesaling. Reebok designs, manufactures and markets 250 models of shoes in twelve footwear categories along with a line of sportswear apparel.

Headquarters: 150 Royall Street Canton, MA 02021

Structure: A public company incorporated in Massachusetts in 1979

Stock Symbol: RBK trades on the New York Stock Exchange with 21,100 shareholders.

Employees: 2,400 non-union employees

Initial Vision: To combine comfort and fashion into function.

Operating Philosophy: To offer products that are new or otherwise superior to the competition.

Hypergrowth: $1 million to $1.9 billion in a decade

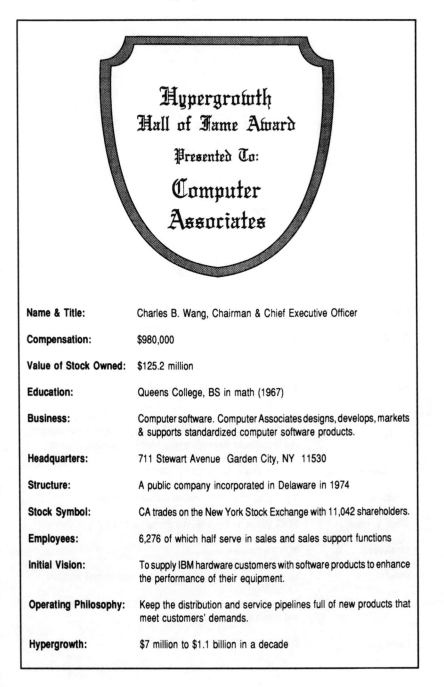

**Hypergrowth
Hall of Fame Award**
Presented To:
**Computer
Associates**

Name & Title: Charles B. Wang, Chairman & Chief Executive Officer

Compensation: $980,000

Value of Stock Owned: $125.2 million

Education: Queens College, BS in math (1967)

Business: Computer software. Computer Associates designs, develops, markets & supports standardized computer software products.

Headquarters: 711 Stewart Avenue Garden City, NY 11530

Structure: A public company incorporated in Delaware in 1974

Stock Symbol: CA trades on the New York Stock Exchange with 11,042 shareholders.

Employees: 6,276 of which half serve in sales and sales support functions

Initial Vision: To supply IBM hardware customers with software products to enhance the performance of their equipment.

Operating Philosophy: Keep the distribution and service pipelines full of new products that meet customers' demands.

Hypergrowth: $7 million to $1.1 billion in a decade

Hypergrowth Hall of Fame Award

Presented To:

Seagate Technology

Name & Title: Alan F. Shugart, Chairman & Chief Executive Officer

Compensation: $4,476,000

Value of Stock Owned: $11.3 million

Education: Redlands University BS in Physics (1953)

Business: Computer accessory manufacturing. Seagate Technology designs, manufactures & markets a broad line of rigid magnetic disc drives for use in computer systems ranging from PC's to supercomputers.

Headquarters: 920 Disc Drive Scotts Valley, CA 95066

Structure: A public company incorporated in Delaware in 1981

Stock Symbol: SGAT trades on the NASDAQ Exchange with 7,713 shareholders.

Employees: 38,000 employees worldwide

Initial Vision: To design and manufacture high quality data storage products.

Operating Philosophy: To be all things to all people by offering products in virtually every size and description.

Hypergrowth: $10 million to $2.4 billion in a decade

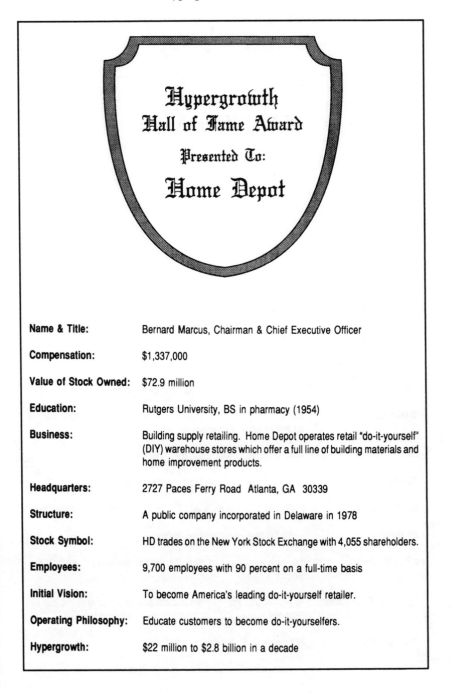

ℌypergrowth
ℌall of ℑame Award

ℜresented ℭo:

ℌome ℜepot

Name & Title: Bernard Marcus, Chairman & Chief Executive Officer

Compensation: $1,337,000

Value of Stock Owned: $72.9 million

Education: Rutgers University, BS in pharmacy (1954)

Business: Building supply retailing. Home Depot operates retail "do-it-yourself" (DIY) warehouse stores which offer a full line of building materials and home improvement products.

Headquarters: 2727 Paces Ferry Road Atlanta, GA 30339

Structure: A public company incorporated in Delaware in 1978

Stock Symbol: HD trades on the New York Stock Exchange with 4,055 shareholders.

Employees: 9,700 employees with 90 percent on a full-time basis

Initial Vision: To become America's leading do-it-yourself retailer.

Operating Philosophy: Educate customers to become do-it-yourselfers.

Hypergrowth: $22 million to $2.8 billion in a decade

**Hypergrowth
Hall of Fame Award
Presented To:
Liz Claiborne**

Name & Title: Elisabeth Claiborne Ortenberg, Chairman, CEO & President

Compensation: $800,000

Value of Stock Owned: $44.3 million

Education: The Academie, did not complete high school

Business: Clothing design and wholesaling. Liz Claiborne, Inc. designs clothing
                         for the needs of career women.

Headquarters: 1441 Broadway New York, NY 10018

Structure: A public company incorporated in Delaware in 1976

Stock Symbol: LIZC trades on the NASDAQ Exchange with 16,195 shareholders.

Employees: 3,400 full-time employees worldwide

Initial Vision: Establish a business to meet the head-to-toe fashion needs of the
                         modern woman.

Operating Philosophy: To neither own nor maintain in-plant equipment so fashions can be
                         designed without the constraints of manufacturing facilities.

Hypergrowth: $79 million to $1.1 billion in a decade

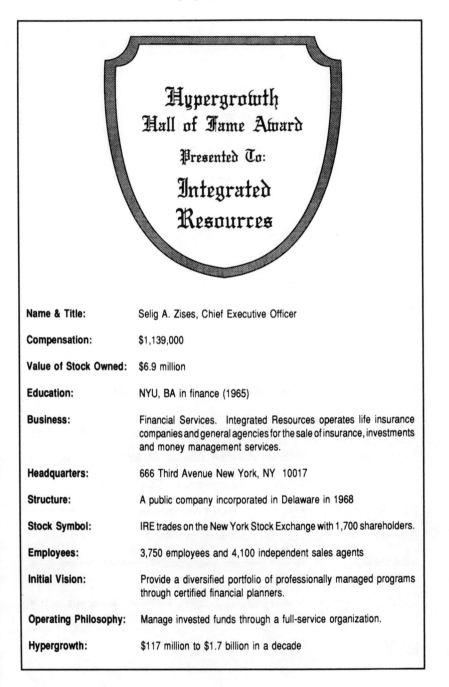

**Hypergrowth
Hall of Fame Award
Presented To:
Integrated
Resources**

Name & Title: Selig A. Zises, Chief Executive Officer

Compensation: $1,139,000

Value of Stock Owned: $6.9 million

Education: NYU, BA in finance (1965)

Business: Financial Services. Integrated Resources operates life insurance companies and general agencies for the sale of insurance, investments and money management services.

Headquarters: 666 Third Avenue New York, NY 10017

Structure: A public company incorporated in Delaware in 1968

Stock Symbol: IRE trades on the New York Stock Exchange with 1,700 shareholders.

Employees: 3,750 employees and 4,100 independent sales agents

Initial Vision: Provide a diversified portfolio of professionally managed programs through certified financial planners.

Operating Philosophy: Manage invested funds through a full-service organization.

Hypergrowth: $117 million to $1.7 billion in a decade

**Hypergrowth
Hall of Fame Award**

Presented To:

Apple Computer

Name & Title:	Steven P. Jobs, Chairman
Compensation:	$339,000
Value of Stock Owned:	$165 million
Education:	Reed College, attended one semester in 1972
Business:	Computer manufacturing. Apple Computer designs, manufactures and sells microprocessor-based PC's & related software and peripherals.
Headquarters:	20525 Mariani Avenue Cupertino, CA 95014
Structure:	A public company incorporated in California in 1977
Stock Symbol:	AAPL trades on the NASDAQ Exchange with 34,266 shareholders.
Employees:	14,517 employees worldwide
Initial Vision:	To make computing power accessible to people by focusing on the individual.
Operating Philosophy:	To make great products, build an exciting work environment, lead the industry in innovation and change the world in the process.
Hypergrowth:	$117 million to $5.3 billion in a decade

𝕳𝖞𝖕𝖊𝖗𝖌𝖗𝖔𝖜𝖙𝖍
𝕳𝖆𝖑𝖑 𝖔𝖋 𝕱𝖆𝖒𝖊 𝕬𝖜𝖆𝖗𝖉

𝕻𝖗𝖊𝖘𝖊𝖓𝖙𝖊𝖉 𝕿𝖔:

𝕿𝖊𝖑𝖊-
𝕮𝖔𝖒𝖒𝖚𝖓𝖎𝖈𝖆𝖙𝖎𝖔𝖓𝖘
𝕴𝖓𝖈.

Name & Title: John C.C. Malone, President & Chief Executive Officer

Compensation: $390,000

Value of Stock Owned: $33.1 million

Education: Yale, BSEE (1963); Johns Hopkins, MS Industrial Management (1964); NYU, MSEE (1965); Johns Hopkins, Ph.D. Operations Research (1967)

Business: Cable television. TCI operates cable systems through its regional divisions & separately managed subsidiaries.

Headquarters: 4643 South Ulster Street Denver, CO 80237

Structure: A public company incorporated in Delaware in 1968

Stock Symbol: TCOMA & TCOMB trade on the NASDAQ Exchange with 4,553 and 955 shareholders, respectively.

Employees: 22,000 with only 225 working from headquarters

Initial Vision: Create a cable channel to compete with networks for advertising revenues.

Operating Philosophy: Maximize cash flow and minimize cash outlay.

Hypergrowth: $135 million to $3.0 billion in a decade

𝕳𝖞𝖕𝖊𝖗𝖌𝖗𝖔𝖜𝖙𝖍
𝕳𝖆𝖑𝖑 𝖔𝖋 𝕱𝖆𝖒𝖊 𝕬𝖜𝖆𝖗𝖉
𝕻𝖗𝖊𝖘𝖊𝖓𝖙𝖊𝖉 𝕿𝖔:
𝕻𝖗𝖎𝖈𝖊 𝕮𝖑𝖚𝖇

Name & Title: Robert E. Price, President & Chief Executive Officer

Compensation: $229,000

Value of Stock Owned: $51.8 million

Education: Claremont College, BA in government (1964)

Business: General merchandise retailing. The Price Club is a cash and carry membership warehouse which sells limited assortment of merchandise below manufacturer suggested retail price.

Headquarters: 2657 Ariane Drive San Diego, CA 92138

Structure: A public company incorporated in California in 1976

Stock Symbol: PCLB trades on the NASDAQ Exchange with 5,231 shareholders.

Employees: 8,516 with one-third on a full-time basis

Initial Vision: Members-only discount warehouse limited to business owners.

Operating Philosophy: Sell goods as cheaply as possible.

Hypergrowth: $146 million to $5.0 billion in a decade

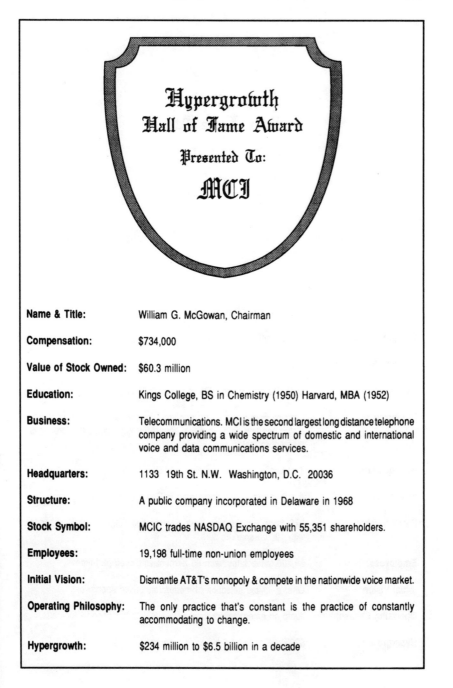

Name & Title: William G. McGowan, Chairman

Compensation: $734,000

Value of Stock Owned: $60.3 million

Education: Kings College, BS in Chemistry (1950) Harvard, MBA (1952)

Business: Telecommunications. MCI is the second largest long distance telephone company providing a wide spectrum of domestic and international voice and data communications services.

Headquarters: 1133 19th St. N.W. Washington, D.C. 20036

Structure: A public company incorporated in Delaware in 1968

Stock Symbol: MCIC trades NASDAQ Exchange with 55,351 shareholders.

Employees: 19,198 full-time non-union employees

Initial Vision: Dismantle AT&T's monopoly & compete in the nationwide voice market.

Operating Philosophy: The only practice that's constant is the practice of constantly accommodating to change.

Hypergrowth: $234 million to $6.5 billion in a decade

Hypergrowth
Hall of Fame Award

Presented To:

The Limited

Name & Title: Leslie H. Wexner, Chairman of the Board

Compensation: $1,154,000

Value of Stock Owned: $1.04 billion

Education: Ohio State University, BA in business (1959)

Business: Clothing manufacturing and retailing. The Limited designs, purchases, distributes and sells women's appare through its 3,095 stores in 9 different formats.

Headquarters: Two Limited Parkway Columbus, OH 43230

Structure: A public company incorporated in Delaware in 1971

Stock Symbol: LTD trades on the New York, London and Tokyo Stock Exchanges with 10,700 shareholders.

Employees: 50,200 "associates" with 60 percent employed part-time

Initial Vision: Offer a limited selection of moderately priced sportswear.

Operating Philosophy: Jump on emerging sportswear trends with low-priced knock-offs.

Hypergrowth: $295 million to $4.6 billion in a decade

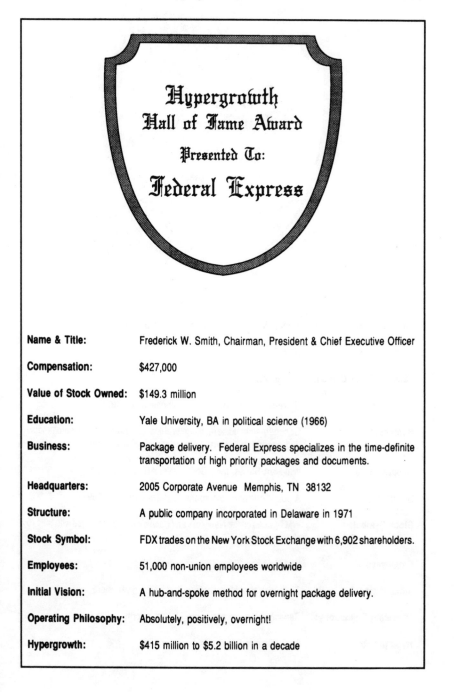

Hypergrowth Hall of Fame Award

Presented To:

Federal Express

Name & Title: Frederick W. Smith, Chairman, President & Chief Executive Officer

Compensation: $427,000

Value of Stock Owned: $149.3 million

Education: Yale University, BA in political science (1966)

Business: Package delivery. Federal Express specializes in the time-definite transportation of high priority packages and documents.

Headquarters: 2005 Corporate Avenue Memphis, TN 38132

Structure: A public company incorporated in Delaware in 1971

Stock Symbol: FDX trades on the New York Stock Exchange with 6,902 shareholders.

Employees: 51,000 non-union employees worldwide

Initial Vision: A hub-and-spoke method for overnight package delivery.

Operating Philosophy: Absolutely, positively, overnight!

Hypergrowth: $415 million to $5.2 billion in a decade

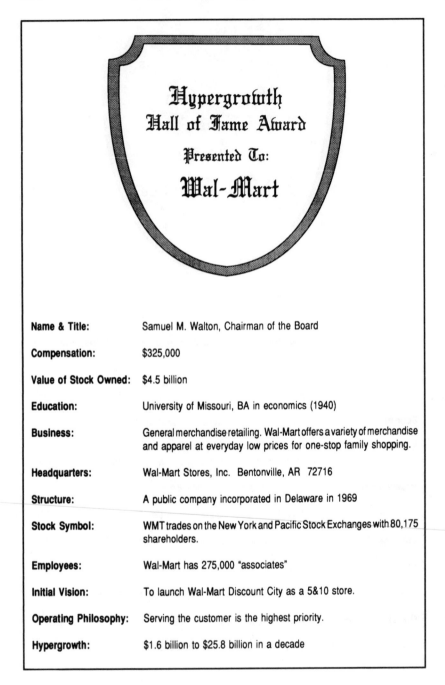

**Hypergrowth
Hall of Fame Award**

Presented To:

Wal-Mart

Name & Title:	Samuel M. Walton, Chairman of the Board
Compensation:	$325,000
Value of Stock Owned:	$4.5 billion
Education:	University of Missouri, BA in economics (1940)
Business:	General merchandise retailing. Wal-Mart offers a variety of merchandise and apparel at everyday low prices for one-stop family shopping.
Headquarters:	Wal-Mart Stores, Inc. Bentonville, AR 72716
Structure:	A public company incorporated in Delaware in 1969
Stock Symbol:	WMT trades on the New York and Pacific Stock Exchanges with 80,175 shareholders.
Employees:	Wal-Mart has 275,000 "associates"
Initial Vision:	To launch Wal-Mart Discount City as a 5&10 store.
Operating Philosophy:	Serving the customer is the highest priority.
Hypergrowth:	$1.6 billion to $25.8 billion in a decade

. . . More Hypergrowth!
(A Scouting Report for the 1990s)

I n the 1980s, hypergrowth was a business anomaly in itself. In the 1990s, however, this anomaly has become a new growth standard as companies continue to achieve hypergrowth.

The 15 companies that established today's hypergrowth benchmark achieved the pinnacle of success in the world of business. Several new companies have generated annual sales of $1 billion or more in relatively short time frames. These enterprises are among the new superstars of business as a result of their remarkable achievements:

- Conner, Inc.
- Sun Microsystems, Inc.
- Home Shopping Network, Inc.
- Blockbuster Entertainment Corporation
- Circuit City Stores, Inc.
- Costco Wholesale, Inc.
- Oracle Systems Corporation
- Nintendo of America, Inc.
- Nike, Inc.
- Microsoft Corporation
- Toys 'R' Us, Inc.
- Office Depot, Inc.

If your company is on the path to hypergrowth or if you know of a company that shows signs of hypergrowth, please fill out the following profile form, and mail it to me.

H. Skip Weitzen
Three Church Circle
Annapolis, Maryland 21401

See you in the Hypergrowth Hall of Fame!

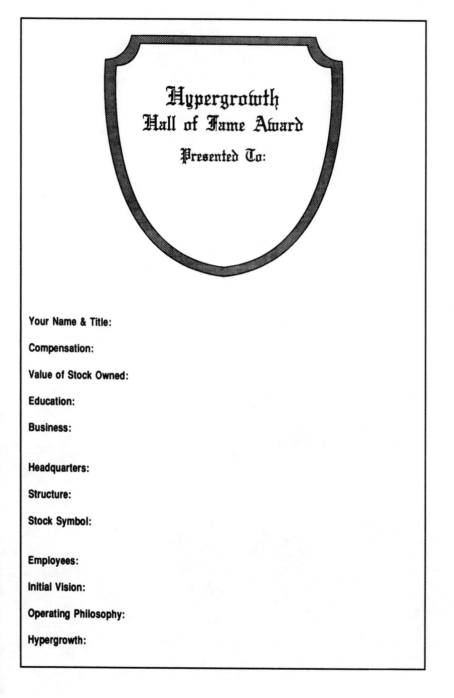

**Hypergrowth
Hall of Fame Award**

Presented To:

Your Name & Title:

Compensation:

Value of Stock Owned:

Education:

Business:

Headquarters:

Structure:

Stock Symbol:

Employees:

Initial Vision:

Operating Philosophy:

Hypergrowth:

Index